Justice and Service Ideas

for Ministry with Young Teens

Heads-up | Easy | Low-Cost | Purposeful

Justice and Service Ideas

for Ministry with Young Teens

Joseph Grant

Heads-up | Easy | Low-Cost | Purposeful

Saint Mary's Press
Christian Brothers Publications
Winona, Minnesota

To Anne, Brendan, Fiona, and Aidan, and those young prophets
who have opened their eyes and my heart to God's transforming justice

Genuine recycled paper with 10% post-consumer waste.
Printed with soy-based ink.

The publishing team included Marilyn Kielbasa, development editor; Cheryl Drivdahl, copy editor; Barbara Bartelson, production editor; Hollace Storkel, typesetter; Cindi Ramm, art director; Kenneth Hey, cover and logo designer; cover images, PhotoDisc Inc.; produced by the graphics division of Saint Mary's Press.

The development consultants for the HELP (Heads-up, Easy, Low-Cost, and Purposeful) series included the following people:

Sarah Bush, Pewee Valley, Kentucky

Jeanne Fairbanks, Tipp City, Ohio

Carole Goodwin, Louisville, Kentucky

Joe Grant, Louisville, Kentucky

Maryann Hakowski, Belleville, Illinois

Jo Joy, Temple, Texas

Kevin Kozlowski, New Carlisle, Ohio

Jennifer MacArthur, Cincinnati, Ohio

David Nissen, Cincinnati, Ohio

Ruthie Nonnenkamp, Prospect, Kentucky

The activities in this book were created by the author and by the following contributors:

Carole Goodwin   Ruthie Nonnenkamp

The acknowledgments continue on page 109.

Printed in the United States of America

Printing: 9 8 7 6 5 4 3 2 1

Year: 2008 07 06 05 04 03 02 01 00

ISBN 0-88489-572-6

Library of Congress Cataloging-in-Publication Data

Grant, Joseph, 1963–
Justice and service ideas for ministry with young teens / Joseph Grant.
        p. cm. — (HELP)
ISBN 0-88489-572-6 (alk. paper)
1. Church work with teenagers—Catholic Church. 2. Christianity and justice—Catholic Church—Study and teaching. 3. Service (Theology)—Study and teaching. I. Title. II. HELP (Series : Winona, Minn.)
BX2347.8.Y7 G76 2000
259'.23—dc21
                                                                        99-050889

Contents

Introduction

Justice and Service Ideas for Ministry with Young Teens is one of seven books in the HELP series—a collection of **H**eads-up, **E**asy, **L**ow-Cost, and **P**urposeful activities for young adolescents. These strategies are designed to be used as part of a comprehensive youth ministry program for grades six to eight. The strategies can stand alone or complement a religious education curriculum.

The other books in the HELP series are as follows:
- *Community-Building Ideas for Ministry with Young Teens* (available in 2001)
- *Family Ideas for Ministry with Young Teens*
- *Hands-on Ideas for Ministry with Young Teens* (available in 2001)
- *Holiday and Seasonal Ideas for Ministry with Young Teens*
- *Prayer Ideas for Ministry with Young Teens*
- *Retreat Ideas for Ministry with Young Teens* (available in 2001)

These books are helpful resources for anyone who works with young adolescents in a church or school setting. They can provide a strong foundation for a year-round, total youth ministry program whose goal is to evangelize young adolescents and support them in their faith journey.

Overview of This Book

Justice and Service Ideas for Ministry with Young Teens may be used by a coordinator of youth ministry, a director of religious education, catechists, teachers, a parish youth ministry team, or any adult who works with young teens. Ownership of the book includes permission to duplicate any part of it for use with program participants.

Some of the strategies in this book are short meeting openers that take no more than 10 minutes. Others are intended to be developed over a period of time. All are designed to foster justice education and attend to the spiritual needs of young teens as growing prophets and disciples.

As they work through these strategies, some young teens may become uncomfortable with experiences and information that challenge the status quo. Some adults in the community may be even *more* uncomfortable with those challenges. Be aware that your efforts to awaken the young people to the deepest meanings of the Gospel may encounter resistance. Also be aware of the life-changing, paradigm-shifting, Reign-building possibilities of those efforts.

Format of the Strategies

Each strategy begins with a brief description of its purpose. The next element is a suggested time for the activity. This is flexible and takes into account several variables, such as the size of the group, the comfort level of the participants, and whether you want to include a break. Use the suggested time as a starting point and modify it according to your circumstances. It is a good idea to include time for a break within the longer strategies.

Next is a description of the size of the group that the strategy was written for. Most of the strategies work with a range of group sizes. If your group is large, be sure to recruit enough adults to help with logistics and supervision. A good rule to follow is that for every six to eight young teens, one adult should be present.

In some strategies a section on special considerations follows the one on group size. It includes things such as notices about remote preparation requirements and cautions to pay special attention to a particular developmental issue of early adolescence.

A complete checklist of materials needed is the next part of the presentation of every strategy. A detailed description of the strategy's procedure is then provided, followed by alternative approaches. Those alternatives may be helpful in adapting the strategy to the needs of your group.

Frequently included is a list of scriptural passages that may be used with the strategy for reflection or prayer. The list is not exhaustive; a Bible concordance will provide additional citations if you want to add a more substantial scriptural component to a strategy.

The final element in each strategy offers space for keeping notes about how you might want to use the strategy in the future or change it to fit the needs of your group.

The final strategy in this collection is different from the others in that it is not a step-by-step procedure for conducting a specific activity. Instead it provides a commentary on the dynamics of involving young people in works of justice and service; ideas for focusing, planning, and deepening the experience of outreach projects; and brief descriptions of strategies you might want to develop.

Programming Ideas

The strategies in this book can be used in a variety of ways. Consider the following suggestions:

◎ The program coordinator, catechists, teachers, and coordinator of youth ministry may collaborate to plan youth meetings and special activities that use strategies from this and other books in the HELP series.

◎ Most of the strategies in this book may be used anytime during the year, either as they are presented or with adaptations. Consider doing some of them in the summer months, when most young adolescents are less busy and may be open to a variety of activities. Youth ministers may use the strategies as part of a strong summer service program for young teens.

◎ Schoolteachers may use ideas from this and other books in the HELP series to supplement their day-to-day curriculum.

◎ Many of the strategies in the HELP series can be adapted for use with multi-generational groups.

Standard Materials

Many of the items in the materials checklists are common to several strategies in the series. To save time consider gathering frequently used materials in convenient bins and storing those bins in a place that is accessible to all staff and volunteer leaders. Some recommendations for how to organize such bins follow.

Supply Bin
The following items frequently appear in materials checklists:

◎ Bibles, at least one for every two participants
◎ masking tape
◎ cellophane tape
◎ washable and permanent markers (thick and thin)
◎ pens or pencils
◎ self-stick notes
◎ scissors
◎ newsprint
◎ blank paper, scrap paper, and notebook paper
◎ postcards
◎ notepaper
◎ envelopes
◎ baskets
◎ candles and matches
◎ items to create a prayer space (e.g., a colored cloth, a cross, a bowl of water, and a vase for flowers)

Craft Bin

Many of the strategies use craft activities to involve the young people. Consider collecting the following supplies in a separate bin:

- construction paper
- yarn and string, in assorted colors
- poster board
- glue and glue sticks
- fabric paints
- glitter and confetti
- used greeting cards
- beads
- modeling clay
- paintbrushes and paints
- crayons
- used magazines and newspapers
- hole punches
- scissors
- stickers of various kinds
- index cards
- gift wrap and ribbon

Music Bin

Young people often find deep and profound meaning in the music and lyrics of songs, both past and present. Also, the right music can set an appropriate mood for a prayer or activity. Begin with a small collection of tapes or CDs in a music bin and add to it over time. You might ask the young people to put some of their favorite music in the bin. The bin might include the following styles of music:

- *Fun gathering music that is neither current nor popular with young teens.* Ideas are well-known classics (e.g., *Overture to William Tell, Stars and Stripes Forever,* and *1812 Overture*), songs from musical theater productions, children's songs, and Christmas songs for use any time of the year.
- *Prayerful, reflective instrumental music, such as the kind that is available in the adult alternative, or New Age, section of music stores.* Labels that specialize in this type of music include Windham Hill and Narada.
- *Popular songs with powerful messages.* If you are not well versed in popular music, ask the young people to offer suggestions.
- *The music of contemporary Christian artists.* Most young teens are familiar with Amy Grant, Michael W. Smith, and Steven Curtis Chapman. Also include the work of Catholic musicians, such as David W. Kauffman, Steve Angrisano, Bruce Deaton, Sarah Hart, Jesse Manibusan, and Jessica Alles.

Other Helpful Resources

In addition to the seven books in the HELP series, the following resources can be useful in your ministry with young adolescents. All the books in the following list are published by Saint Mary's Press and can be obtained by calling or writing us at the phone number and address listed in the "Your Comments or Suggestions" section at the end of this introduction.

The Catholic Youth Bible, edited by Brian Singer-Towns (2000). The most youth-friendly Bible for Catholic teens available. The scriptural text is accompanied by hundreds of articles to help young people pray, study, and live the Scriptures.

Faith Works for Junior High: Scripture- and Tradition-Based Sessions for Faith Formation, by Lisa-Marie Calderone-Stewart (1993). A series of twelve active meeting plans on various topics related to the Scriptures and church life.

Guided Meditations for Junior High: Good Judgment, Gifts, Obedience, Inner Blindness, by Jane E. Ayer (1997). Four guided meditations for young teens, available on audiocassette or compact disc. A leader's guide includes the script and programmatic options. Other volumes in this series, called A Quiet Place Apart, will also work with young teens.

Looking Past the Sky: Prayers by Young Teens, edited by Marilyn Kielbasa (1999). A collection of 274 prayers by and for young adolescents in grades six to eight.

One-Day Retreats for Junior High Youth, by Geri Braden-Whartenby and Joan Finn Connelly (1997). Six retreats that each fit into a school day or an afternoon or evening program. Each retreat contains a variety of icebreakers, prayers, group exercises, affirmations, and guided meditations.

Prayers with Pizzazz for Junior High Teens, by Judi Lanciotti (1996). A variety of creative prayer experiences that grab young teens' attention. The prayers are useful in many different settings, such as classes, meetings, prayer services, and retreats.

ScriptureWalk Junior High: Bible Themes, by Maryann Hakowski (1999). Eight 90-minute sessions to help bring youth and the Bible together. Each session applies biblical themes to the life issues that concern young teens.

Catechism Connection for Teens collection, by Lisa Calderone-Stewart and Ed Kunzman (1999).
That First Kiss and Other Stories
My Wish List and Other Stories
Better Than Natural and Other Stories
Straight from the Heart and Other Stories
Meeting Frankenstein and Other Stories
The five books in this collection contain short, engaging stories for teens on the joys and struggles of adolescent life, each story with a reflection connecting it to a Catholic Christian belief. Each book's faith connections

reflect teachings from a different part of the *Catechism of the Catholic Church.*

Two other books, both published by Free Spirit Publishing in Minneapolis and distributed by Saint Mary's Press, may be particularly helpful supplements to *Justice and Service Ideas for Ministry with Young Teens.* Both of these books are useful for religious education groups and Confirmation candidates as well as youth ministry programs.

The Kid's Guide to Service Projects: Over Five Hundred Service Ideas for Young People Who Want to Make a Difference, by Barbara A. Lewis (1995). Hundreds of service ideas in areas like literacy, the environment, hunger, politics, and animals.

The Kid's Guide to Social Action: How to Solve the Social Problems You Choose— and Turn Creative Thinking into Positive Action, by Barbara A. Lewis (1991, rev. 1998). A guide to help young people turn creative thinking into positive action. Includes tips on things like Internet research, media coverage, surveys, and petitions.

Connections to the Discovering Program

The Discovering Program, published by Saint Mary's Press, is a religious education program for young people in grades six to eight. It consists of fourteen six-session minicourses. Each session is 1 hour long and based on the principles of active learning.

The strategies in the HELP series cover themes that are loosely connected to those explored by the Discovering Program, and can be used as part of a total youth ministry program in which the Discovering curriculum is the central catechetical component. However, no strategy in the series presumes that the participants have taken a particular course in the Discovering Program, or requires that they do so. The appendices at the end of this book list the connections between the HELP strategies and the Discovering courses.

Your Comments or Suggestions

Saint Mary's Press wants to know your reactions to the strategies in the HELP series. We are also interested in new youth ministry strategies for use with young teens. If you have a comment or suggestion, please write the series editor, Marilyn Kielbasa, at 702 Terrace Heights, Winona, MN 55987-1320; call the editor at our toll-free number, 800-533-8095; or e-mail the editor at *mkielbasa@smp.org.* Your ideas will help improve future editions of these books.

Label Makers

OVERVIEW This activity uses a soup can label as a symbol to help the young people recognize intolerance and see more deeply into themselves and others. It also provides a format to address the broad implications of stereotyping, and challenges the young teens to look for the Christian response to it.

Suggested Time

35 to 45 minutes

Group Size

This strategy works best with a group of twelve or more.

Special Considerations

This activity requires the young teens to take some risks. It works best when the group members have achieved a certain level of comfort with one another, ideally after the group has met regularly over a period of time.

Even if the group members know one another well and have good self-esteem, they may not be comfortable wearing randomly distributed labels in procedure step 3. You might want to invite the participants to read their labels silently and then discuss them without pinning them on. Or add some control by distributing the labels carefully rather than randomly, avoiding any obvious problems such as giving the label "Heavy" to a young person who is overweight.

Materials Needed

- ☼ notepaper, envelopes, and stamps
- ☼ newsprint or poster board, and a marker
- ☼ masking tape
- ☼ one can of soup
- ☼ thin-line permanent markers, one for each person
- ☼ safety pins, one for each person
- ☼ a can opener
- ☼ a jar or bowl

PROCEDURE

Preparation. Well before you meet for this session, send a note to each person, inviting him or her to bring a can of soup. Bring one additional can of soup yourself.

Write the following phrase and list of words on a piece of newsprint or poster board. These represent stereotypical labels that young people often use. You may wish to substitute terms that are more common in your area or more appropriate for your participants. Avoid anything that might be racially or sexually offensive. If you have more than twelve people in your group, you may wish to add more labels. You could also repeat labels.

You are . . .

1. weird	5. dumb	9. slow
2. cute	6. cool	10. short
3. a nerd	7. heavy	11. a klutz
4. a dork	8. smart	12. a loser

Post the list where the young people will notice it as they enter the room.

1. As the young people enter the room for the session, make a mental note of their responses to the list you have posted. Direct everyone to stack their cans of soup in a designated location. Add the can that you brought. Then secretly remove one can from the stack, making sure that the young people do not see you doing so. Carefully remove the label from this can and return the can to the stack. (If another adult is present, you might ask her or him to attend to this task quietly while the young people are otherwise occupied.)

2. Give each person a thin-line permanent marker and a safety pin. Tell the participants each to take a can from the stack and to make a small mark on its bottom, identifying themselves and the can's contents. You might suggest that they use their initials and an abbreviation, such as "AG tom" for "Amy Green, tomato soup," or any other marking that they will recognize and understand later. Then direct them to remove the label carefully, using the safety pin, and return the unlabeled can to the pile.

3. Assign each person a number that corresponds to one of the numbers on the newsprint list. Direct the young people to write the word from the list on the blank side of their soup can label and put the label facedown in a pile in the center of the group. When everyone has added their label to the pile, distribute the labels randomly, and direct the young people to use their safety pin to attach their label to their clothing in an obvious place. Note that the label should be pinned so that the word written on the back is facing out.

4. In the large group, discuss the young peoples' reactions to the labels they were given. The following questions may be useful discussion-starters:

Does your label fit?

Is it a good description of who you really are?

Which of the names listed would you least want to be called?

Do you know anyone who fits perfectly into one of the listed categories?

Have you ever been referred to by one of these descriptions?

Which of these descriptions have you used when referring to another person?

Which of these names do you believe can be used as appropriate descriptions for a person?

Do you find any of these names offensive or inappropriate?

Did anyone come to mind as you read these names?

Do you believe labels are necessary when you are getting to know or relating with people?

5. Invite the young teens to return to the stack of unlabeled cans and retrieve the can they marked earlier. Ask them each to tell the group the contents of their can.

The can that you altered at the beginning of the session will be unclaimed. Place this mystery can in front of the group. Pass the can around the group and ask the participants to guess its contents. Then open the mystery can and place the contents in a jar or bowl.

6. Present the following ideas in your own words:

Let's take some time to reflect on the meaning of the symbols used in the exercise:

The labels are symbols of the things that stop us from welcoming, listening to, and caring about others.

The mystery can is a reminder that only God knows who we really are inside.

The can opener represents friendship, which opens people up and reveals the goodness in each one.

Think about how you are treated by those who do not know you, and how you treat others. Remember that no one can know what is inside a person until they build a relationship with that person. Labeling people leads us to be judgmental, close-minded, and close-hearted.

In life we do not get to choose how others label us, but we can choose how we respond to others and how we welcome and accept them. Only God knows the potential that lies within each person.

7. Remove the newsprint list and put it on the floor in the middle of the group. Tell the participants to remove one another's labels and place them in a pile on top of the newsprint. Conclude by reading Ps. 139:1–18,23–24 prayerfully.

ALTERNATIVE APPROACHES

◎ Reattach the labels to the cans, or make new labels to identify the contents of the cans clearly, and donate the soup to a food program.

◎ If you have extra time, add this step before the closing prayer: Invite the group to name the kinds of people who are most often labeled or stereotyped by society. For example, they might name those who are minorities, foreigners, physically or mentally challenged, of different sexual orientation, homeless, and poor. Then ask the young people to list the kinds of people most often labeled and stereotyped in Jesus' time, and discuss how Jesus responded to them. Use the following Gospel excerpts for this list and discussion:

  ◎ *Foreigners and women.* John 4:6–10 (A Samaritan woman at a well)
  ◎ *Lepers and social outcasts.* Matt. 8:1–4 (A leper touched and cured by Jesus)
  ◎ *Criminals and public sinners.* Luke 23:39–43 (The good thief crucified with Jesus); John 8:1–11 (A woman caught in adultery)
  ◎ *The disabled and the mentally ill.* Matt. 9:1–8 (The cure of a lame person); Mark 5:1–13 (The cure of a man possessed by evil)
  ◎ *The simple and poor.* Matt. 11:25–30 (Jesus' welcome for the poor); Mark 10:46–52 (Jesus' cure for a blind beggar)

◎ Challenge the young teens to create a poster with a slogan about the dangers of stereotyping. Add the labels from their soup cans and some scriptural quotes. Hang the poster in the youth room or church hall.

◎ Ask the young people to make signs for the meeting space to remind the group that labeling is prohibited. Use the common symbol of a red circle with a slash as an example.

- Invite the young people to write prayers, reflections, poems, or rap songs about the influence of labels and stereotypes.
- As part of the closing prayer, tell the young people to write on the labels they removed from one another the names of people who have suffered discrimination. Offer a prayer for the victims of racism, ageism, sexism, and other stereotypes.

SCRIPTURAL CONNECTIONS

- Lev. 25:35 (Care for the outcast and foreigner.)
- Matt. 5:22 (Anyone who insults another will be condemned.)
- Matt. 7:1–5 (Do not judge.)
- Matt. 7:12 (Treat others as you would like them to treat you.)
- Rom. 15:7 (Accept one another as Christ accepts us.)

NOTES

Use the space below to jot notes and reminders for the next time you use this strategy.

The Peacemaker Award: In Recognition of Gospel Greatness

This activity introduces real-life stories of Gospel commitment, presents Christian role models, and allows the young people to celebrate in a creative way the lives of peacemakers. It is ideal for retreats or youth group meetings, as a Confirmation project, or as a parishwide event.

Suggested Time

The time is variable, depending on the number of awards and the number of people involved. If you are doing the activity with a small group, it can be completed in about an hour. If you are involving the whole parish, you may want to spread the process out over several weeks.

Group Size

This activity works with any size group. If you have a large number of participants, they can be divided into small task groups.

Special Considerations

The awards will have a greater impact if the entire parish is involved in the selection process. However, the activity will also work with a small group of young people. Before you begin the process, decide who will be involved and how much time you want to devote.

Materials Needed

:☼: a Bible

:☼: newsprint and markers (optional)

:☼: materials for creating the awards (see the procedure section titled What Will the Award Look Like?)

:☼: supplies for presenting the awards (see the procedure section titled How Will the Awards Be Presented?)

PROCEDURE

Whether you conduct this activity with a small group of young adolescents or make it a parishwide event, three questions must be answered by the group:

Who Will Get the Award?

1. Read Matt. 20:25–28. Introduce the idea of the Peacemaker Award to the group by explaining that it is to be given to people who live out their commitment to the Gospel. The award is intended to challenge the popular concept of celebrity—that is, wealth, beauty, power, and strength—and focus instead on signs of integrity and Gospel living.

Discuss with the young people their understanding of the characteristics of a peacemaker and develop some guidelines for nomination. You might list on newsprint a number of adjectives that describe a peacemaker, such as the ones that follow:

◎ humble

◎ caring

◎ committed

◎ courageous

◎ compassionate

◎ selfless

◎ reconciling

◎ generous

You might also list Christian acts of mercy, such as these:

◎ feeding the hungry

◎ clothing the cold and naked

◎ visiting the sick or imprisoned

◎ sheltering the homeless

◎ welcoming the lonely stranger

2. Determine how many people will be given the award and whether the nominees should be local people or people from a broader region, such as a surrounding metropolitan area or your state. Then, based on the guidelines, invite the participants to think about whom to nominate for the award. If you are conducting this process over a period of time, you might ask the young people to consult their parents, parish staff, teachers, or other adults for ideas.

3. After the group has had a chance to think about the nominations, list the names of their candidates on newsprint. Ask the young people to give reasons for their choices by referring to the guidelines.

4. Invite the entire group to discuss the nominations, then determine the winners. You might conduct a secret ballot during which each person votes for his or her top three choices. Tally the results and award the top vote getters.

What Will the Award Look Like?

Brainstorm a variety of creative options for the award itself, then choose one or more of those ideas and make an award for each recipient. Some possibilities are listed below. Any of them can be combined.

◎ Create a Gospel Greatness certificate or poster for each recipient, with the recipient's name, decorated with biblical quotes, words of appreciation, the rationale for the recognition, and descriptions of the recipient's Gospel greatness.

◎ Declare a Peace Day in celebration of the Gospel greatness of the award winners.

◎ Plant a tree or shrub in honor of the just witness of each recipient.

◎ Set aside a wall or bulletin board that features individuals whom the young people look on and celebrate as Gospel greats.

◎ Choose or create for each recipient a symbol of faith (such as a large candle or a wooden or clay cross, dove, or heart), decorate it, and all sign it (or select someone to sign it from the group).

◎ Create a peace banner or quilt. Use colored cloth and fabric paint or markers, and decorate it with the names of the recipients.

How Will the Awards Be Presented?

Decide how the young people will present the awards, spread the word, and publicly recognize the recipients. Some ideas follow. Many of them can be combined.

◎ Host an honor banquet and invite the winners. Ask the Peacemaker Award recipients to share a few words with the young people.

◎ Announce the awards at a weekly Mass, and ask the celebrant and the young people to do a ritual blessing of the recipients.

◎ Announce the Peacemaker Awards as part of a regular school awards day.

ALTERNATIVE APPROACHES

◎ *Gospel Greats Versus Hollywood Greats.* For maximum contrast with popular conceptions of celebrity, stage the announcement of the Peacemaker Awards to coincide with that of the Oscars, the Emmys, or other popular awards.

◎ *Comparative Idols.* Make a list of the most recognized stars of music, sports, and entertainment. Invite the young teens to share their knowledge about the personalities and lifestyles of those icons. Compare their observations with the guidelines the group came up with for judging Gospel greatness.

◎ *Saints Alive.* Invite the young people to choose and research radical Christian witnesses from the past or present, whose message is important for youth today. Challenge them to focus on models of just living and to identify local prophets and living saints.

SCRIPTURAL CONNECTIONS

The following scriptural references can be used with any part of this activity:
◎ Psalm 131 (My heart is not proud.)
◎ Isa. 58:6–11 (This is what God asks—that you shelter the poor; then your light will shine.)
◎ Matt. 18:1–4 (Who is the greatest in the Reign of God?)
◎ Mark 9:34–37 (Those who want to be first must make themselves servants of all.)
◎ John 13:1–15 (If I, the Lord, have washed your feet, you should wash one another's feet.)

NOTES

Use the space below to jot notes and reminders for the next time you use this strategy.

Youth Can

The young people decorate a large trash can to increase the parish's or school's awareness of youth outreach activities and to collect cash donations or items for a variety of youth-sponsored service projects.

Suggested Time

The time will depend on the creativity of the group. The young people can easily decorate a trash can during a religious education class or youth group meeting. However, if they use materials that require drying time, it may be advisable to spread the activity over a longer period.

Group Size

This activity will work with any size group, but it may be necessary to divide a large group into teams responsible for various tasks.

Special Considerations

◎ If you have a large parish, you may want to make more than one Youth Can to place at strategic points on the property.
◎ Consider asking a local hardware or home-and-garden store to donate the necessary materials.
◎ You may want to tell the young people that they should wear old clothes for painting.
◎ If you are using paint, be sure to do the work outside or in a well-ventilated room.

Materials Needed

This project can be simple or elaborate, and the supplies needed will vary accordingly. Because the Youth Can needs to be eye-catching, it is important that it be brightly decorated. The basic supplies are listed below; feel free to add other items, such as pictures, streamers, rope, and colored tape.

- ☀ poster board or colored paper
- ☀ permanent markers in various colors
- ☀ scissors
- ☀ a large plastic trash can, with wheels if possible
- ☀ spray paint, or cans of paint and brushes (optional)
- ☀ tape
- ☀ drop cloths or old newspapers

PROCEDURE

1. Present the idea of the Youth Can as a mobile collection unit and billboard that will promote the concept of Christian service and involve the whole parish or school in the outreach activities of the group throughout the year. The Youth Can might be used for a variety of donated items, such as clothing for migrant workers, canned goods for a food pantry, fans during the summer months for shut-ins, blankets or toiletries for a homeless shelter, monetary donations for a designated charity or program, and supplies for the youth program.

2. Decide with the group where to put the Youth Can. It should be in a high-traffic area so that it will be noticed by as many people as possible. For example, the Youth Can could be placed in the gathering area of the church, with information on current service projects.

Brainstorm possibilities for an outreach project to inaugurate the Youth Can, and decide which one to pursue.

3. Ask the group to create a slogan that communicates the message that young people care, share, and live out their Gospel call to serve others. An example of such a slogan is "Youth can care. So can you." Recruit volunteers to create a poster of the slogan.

Also invite the young people to search for scriptural passages that promote sharing and serving. Some passages are listed at the end of this plan; you might use them to give the participants a place to start. Ask for volunteers to create small posters of selected passages.

4. Display a large trash can and brainstorm various ways to decorate it so that it will be a highly noticeable and an informative tool. Consider painting the can. Include the posters of the slogan and scriptural passages, and an assortment of other decorations for the group to choose from. If you are spreading this project out over a period of time, you might assign the young people to bring in specific decorating supplies that they would like to use.

Before any paint or decoration is applied, spread drop cloths or old newspapers to protect the area, and ensure that everyone is aware of the plan. Monitor the activity carefully, especially if the young people are using paint or other messy materials.

5. Discuss with the group ways to advertise the Youth Can. You might put something in the parish bulletin, youth newsletter, or local media. If the option is open in your parish, you could invite young people to make announcements at liturgy.

SCRIPTURAL CONNECTIONS

The following scriptural passages may be used to decorate the Youth Can, and posters or flyers that explain and announce its purpose:
- Ps. 37:21 (The righteous person is generous.)
- Prov. 28:27 (Those who give to the poor will never want.)
- Isa. 58:7–8 (Share with others; then your light will shine.)
- Matt. 10:8 (Give of yourself freely.)
- Luke 12:33–34 (Where your treasure is, there will your heart be.)
- Luke 12:15 (Life is not measured by possessions.)

NOTES

Use the space below to jot notes and reminders for the next time you use this strategy.

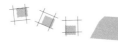

A Place at Our Table

OVERVIEW This strategy is intended to raise awareness of the reality of hunger in our nation and world. Creating a place mat for their family's dining table allows the young people each to take home a vivid reminder of the scandal of starvation and malnutrition in a world of plenty. Their families are challenged to respond by making a place at their table and in their life for those who struggle with hunger.

Suggested Time

About 90 minutes

Group Size

This activity can be done with any size group.

Materials Needed

- ☼ table knives, one for every four to six people
- ☼ a hard surface such as a piece of poster board, if needed (see procedure step 1)
- ☼ newsprint and a marker
- ☼ masking tape
- ☼ small bowls or paper plates, one for each person
- ☼ large bowls of popcorn, one for every four to six people
- ☼ teaspoons
- ☼ Styrofoam or paper cups, one for every four to six people
- ☼ copies of handout 1, "Hunger in a World of Plenty," one for each person
- ☼ a Bible (optional)

☼ 12-by-18-inch pieces of poster board, one for each person
☼ a variety of art supplies, such as scissors, markers or paints, used magazines, and colored paper
☼ clear self-adhesive paper (optional)

PROCEDURE

Preparation. On newsprint, list the following questions:
◎ What is your favorite food, and when was the last time you enjoyed it?
◎ When was the last time you ate so much that you were stuffed?
◎ What kind or kinds of junk food do you tend to eat too much of?
◎ What foods do you crave?
◎ When was the last time you missed a meal and were really hungry?
◎ What is your least favorite food, and how do you deal with it when it is on your plate?
◎ What is your idea of a perfect breakfast?
◎ If you had to do without one type of food that you regularly eat, what would you want it to be?

Post the newsprint where everyone can see it.

You may want to create a sample place mat or two, as described in procedure step 7, to demonstrate some options to the young teens.

1. Form groups of four, five, or six young people and direct them to sit in a circle. Put a table knife in the middle of each circle. Provide a hard surface such as a sheet of poster board if the knife is on carpet, and give the following instructions in your own words:

Someone in each group is to spin the knife. When the knife stops, the person it is pointing at is to answer one of the questions listed on newsprint. Then someone else in the group is to spin the knife, and so on.

Allow this activity to go on for about 5 minutes.

2. Give each person a small bowl or paper plate. Place in the middle of each group the following items:
◎ a large bowl of popped popcorn
◎ one teaspoon if the group has four members, or two teaspoons if it has five or six members
◎ one Styrofoam or paper cup

Direct the participants to pick up one of the items from the center of their group. One or two people in each group will be left without anything. Tell the young people not to eat the popcorn until directed to do so.

3. Lead the group through the following process of distributing the popcorn, waiting until one step is completed before moving on to the next:

1. The person with a cup takes two heaping cupfuls of popcorn from the large bowl and empties them into her or his small bowl or plate.
2. The person or people who did not take anything from the center of the circle take one handful of popcorn and empty it into their small bowl or plate.
3. The person or people with a teaspoon scoop out as many pieces of popcorn as will fit on the spoon and put them into their small bowl or plate.
4. The person holding the large bowl of popcorn places the bowl in the center of the group without taking any for herself or himself.

4. Distribute copies of handout 1 and read some of its information with the young people. Point out that the statistics represent the reality of hunger on a global scale. In a world of six billion people, one billion are forced to struggle with hunger and starvation every day.

5. Remove the large bowls with the surplus popcorn from each group, and ask the groups to talk about the unjust distribution of popcorn and come up with some way for each member of the group to have enough.

6. Read or tell the story of Lazarus and the wealthy man (Luke 16:19–31). Lead the young people in a discussion of the following questions:

What do you think Jesus is telling us in this story?

How could the rich man fail to notice a starving man at his gate?

Where do hungry people live, and who helps them?

Why are there so many starving people in a world where some have more than they really need?

What can you do to remind yourself and others to stop, and notice and share with those who are starving?

7. Announce that the young people will each have a chance to take the lessons that they have learned about global hunger home to their family by making a place mat for the family table. Display one or two sample place mats if you have made them.

Distribute a piece of poster board to each person. Make available other art supplies. Allow the young people about 45 minutes to create an eye-catching place mat for their family table. Encourage them to invent slogans, use scriptural quotes, and add statistics from the handout.

If you have clear self-adhesive paper available, help the young people cover their place mats to protect them from spills.

8. Invite the young teens to show their creations to one another and explain them. Conclude with a prayer for the people who suffer from hunger in a world of plenty. End your prayer with these words from the Magnificat: "You have filled the hungry with good things and sent the rich away empty" (adapted from Luke 1:53).

Encourage the young teens to take their place mat home, explain it to their family, and use it at their table as a reminder to share their daily bread with others.

ALTERNATIVE APPROACHES

- Use this activity as a project for Lent or Thanksgiving. Suggest to the young people's families that they set an extra place at their table, put an empty plate on the place mat, and fill the plate with canned or packaged food, or money, which they then donate to a service agency.
- Display the place mats in the parish or school foyer or youth room, or put together a more elaborate exhibit involving a table, the place mats, and place settings. Place a basket or box below or near the exhibit, for the collection of food donations.
- Use the place mats as part of a prayer service. Invite the young people to bring canned goods to the session. At the end of the session, pile the donated food on the place mats in the center of the room. Read the story of the loaves and the fishes (John 6:1–13), and conclude with a prayer for those who are hungry. Donate the canned goods to the local pantry.
- Make place mats to send to local and national leaders to challenge them to share national resources and increase aid to countries struggling with malnutrition.
- Include this strategy as part of a family night for the young teens and their parents, brothers and sisters, and other relatives.

SCRIPTURAL CONNECTIONS

- Isa. 58:7 (Share your food with the hungry.)
- Luke 6:24–25 (The rich will go hungry.)
- Luke 6:38 (To those who give, much will be given.)
- Luke 14:13 (When you give a feast, invite those who have little.)
- James 2:14–17 (Faith must be accompanied by action.)

NOTES

Use the space below to jot notes and reminders for the next time you use this strategy.

Hunger in a World of Plenty

✳ Across the world starvation and malnutrition cause the needless deaths of children, women, and men at alarming rates:
   - Eighteen million people die every year.
   - Almost fifty thousand people die every day.
   - Over two thousand people die every hour.
   - More than thirty-four people die every minute.
   - More than eight people die every fifteen seconds.
   (*Catholic Social Teaching and Human Rights,* page F-4.)

✳ One-half of the children's deaths around the world are related to hunger (*Catholic Social Teaching and Human Rights,* page F-3).

✳ Chronic hunger is a daily reality for 34.7 million people in the United States of America (*Catholic Social Teaching and Human Rights,* page F-3).

✳ To provide basic health care and nutrition for everyone in impoverished countries would cost approximately thirteen billion dollars more than is currently being spent; seventeen billion dollars is spent each year on pet food in the United States and Europe (*Celebrate Jubilee and Justice!*).

✳ An estimated 700 million people in impoverished countries suffer chronic hunger (*Operation Rice Bowl Lenten Program*).

✳ One billion people worldwide—one-sixth of the total population—are forced to live on less than one dollar a day and suffer starvation and malnutrition (*Operation Rice Bowl Lenten Program*).

✳ The world consumes six times more goods and services today than it did in 1950, but over one billion people still lack basic needs (*Celebrate Jubilee and Justice!*).

✳ The United States gives less than 1 percent of its total budget as financial aid to impoverished countries (*Operation Rice Bowl Lenten Program*).

(The data in this list comes from *Catholic Social Teaching and Human Rights: An Educational Packet,* by Jane Deren, Marissa Maurer, and Julie Vieira [Washington, DC: Center of Concern, 1998], pages F-3 and F-4, copyright © 1998; *Celebrate Jubilee and Justice!* by the Center of Concern [Washington, DC: Center of Concern, 1999], page 10, copyright © 1999; and *Operation Rice Bowl Lenten Program,* by Catholic Relief Services [Baltimore, MD: Catholic Relief Services, 1998], pages 21–22.)

Peacebreak: A Calendar of Peace and Justice

OVERVIEW

This activity helps the young teens gain a faith-based perspective on human history by creating a calendar that highlights momentous occasions in which peace or justice has "broken out," and celebrating the lives of the people who have worked for a just world.

Suggested Time

This strategy should be done over a period of time to allow for research and development of the calendar. You will need 45 to 60 minutes to plan the format and distribution of tasks, time to gather dates and names, and 60 to 90 minutes to create the calendar.

Group Size

This strategy can be done with any size group.

Materials Needed

- ☼ a variety of historical resources, such as books, movies, and artwork
- ☼ newsprint and a marker
- ☼ supplies for creating a calendar, such as poster board, scissors, and colored markers

PROCEDURE

Preparation. Gather a variety of historical resources from a local library and the Internet. Accounts and depictions should span a wide timeline of human history. Display these items in the gathering space.

Label the top of a sheet of newsprint, "Both sides of the story." Draw a line down the middle of the paper.

1. As the young people arrive, invite them to browse the historical items that you have displayed in the gathering space. Then lead the group in a discussion of the following questions:

What kinds of historical events and people are most often depicted in the media?

What is your favorite historical movie or story? Why?

If you could live at any other time in history, what era would you choose? Why?

If you could be a historical figure from the past, who would you be?

What are some important historical dates that you have memorized?

On the newsprint you have prepared, categorize the young people's responses according to the themes they highlight. List events such as outbreaks of war, destruction, disasters, invasion, and famine on one half of the paper, and outbreaks of peace, missions of mercy or relief, and declarations of justice, equality, and human rights on the other.

2. Point out that history is told most often as a story of domination, exploitation, or destruction. Introduce the idea of a calendar that commemorates the other side of the human story. Invite the young people to do their own research into human history, gathering information on events such as peace movements, the endings of wars, declarations of human rights, and the activities of great peacemakers. Explain that they will create a one-year calendar that includes a brief description of each event on the day of the year when it occurred or is commemorated. You might want to use the following examples to give the young people an idea of the scope of the calendar. Note that countless other dates and events might be included.

◎ *1 January.* The International World Day of Peace is celebrated.

◎ *8 May.* The Second World War in Europe ended on this day in 1945.

◎ *2 October.* Mohandas K. Gandhi, "the Mahatma (Great Soul) of India," was born on this day in 1869.

◎ *11 November.* On this day in 1918, the armistice that ended the First World War was declared in France.

◎ *18 December.* On this day in 1865, the Thirteenth Amendment to the U.S. Constitution was ratified, abolishing slavery.

Discuss the format of the calendar. It could be a monthly wall hanging, a twelve-month poster, a timeline poster, or even a weekly listing that gets published in the parish bulletin or posted on the school bulletin board.

Consider assigning the young people to small groups working on individual months or periods in history. Encourage them to use all the resources they can find, such as materials from the public and school libraries, articles from the Internet, almanacs, and peace and justice publications. Let them know how much time they will have for the research. Designate a working period that allows them to study their topic in some depth without losing focus, perhaps one to two weeks.

3. After the young people have completed their research, lead the group in compiling the calendar. Provide the necessary materials and supervise the participants' work.

4. When the calendar is done, gather the group and note the following points in your own words:

A number of people have been inspired throughout history to dedicate their lives to the pursuit of justice and peace. This challenges the validity of a history that overemphasizes war and destruction, and presents a perspective of history rooted in our faith that God's love is active in our human story.

5. Conclude with a brief prayer service focusing on giving thanks for the men and women who work tirelessly for peace and justice, and asking for God's help in becoming one of those people. You might include a litany of the people named in the calendar, with each name followed by the invocation, "Pray for us."

ALTERNATIVE APPROACHES

◎ The calendar could work well as a yearlong project in which the young teens research dates each month and complete the calendar as the year progresses.
◎ If the calendar is done creatively, it could be printed or reproduced as a fundraiser for youth service events or agencies that the young teens have sponsored.
◎ Distribute copies of the calendar among the young teens to use with their families or in their schools.
◎ Display the calendar in the youth room, parish hallway, church entryway, or school lobby, to serve as a visual aid for justice education.
◎ Select excerpts from the calendar and publish them in youth newsletters or the parish bulletin.

SCRIPTURAL CONNECTIONS

- ◎ Isa. 52:7 (How beautiful are the feet of the messengers of peace.)
- ◎ Jer. 29:11–14 (The plans I have for you are for peace, not disaster.)
- ◎ Amos 5:24 (Let justice flow like a river.)
- ◎ Matt. 5:9 (Blessed are the peacemakers.)
- ◎ 1 Cor. 14:33 (God is a God of peace.)
- ◎ 2 Cor. 13:11 (Live in peace.)

NOTES

Use the space below to jot notes and reminders for the next time you use this strategy.

Christian Coupons

OVERVIEW

This hands-on strategy offers the young teens an opportunity to increase their awareness of the influence of consumerism, engage in a service activity, and act as agents of charity within their families, parish, and neighborhoods.

Suggested Time

About 1 hour to create the coupons, plus time to distribute the coupons and to collect and distribute the goods.

Group Size

This strategy can be done with any size group.

Materials Needed

- ☼ "Buy one, get one free" store ads and posters
- ☼ masking tape
- ☼ a tape player, or a television and VCR (optional)
- ☼ paper
- ☼ pens or pencils
- ☼ black markers of various thicknesses
- ☼ card stock

PROCEDURE

Preparation. Collect store ads and posters that say, "Buy one, get one free," and post them throughout the meeting place.

Well before the meeting, ask a few young people to gather a variety of grocery store coupons from newspapers and stores. Direct them to search for "buy one, get one free" coupons in particular. You might also ask some young people to make an audio or video recording of several television or radio commercials.

1. Invite the young people to share briefly the coupons they have collected, and open a discussion on how the messages and values of commercialism affect daily life. If people recorded commercials, play them at this time.

2. Ask the young people to respond to the following questions:

What is your favorite commercial?

When you buy clothes or food, do you always buy the least expensive product? Why or why not?

How many of you are wearing something with a name-brand label? Count the total number of labels on clothing, shoes, and accessories in your group.

Have you ever tried to count the number of messages (print, audio, and visual) that you are exposed to on your trip to school each day?

When have you gone into a store to buy something specific and left with more than that?

3. Point out that the commercial invitation to "buy one, get one free" often encourages people to purchase more than they need. Tell the young people to examine the language, message, and style of the "buy one, get one free" coupons that were shared earlier. Announce that they will create "Christian coupons"—"buy two, give one away" coupons that encourage people to shop for food items for themselves and for others. Explain that the group will use those coupons in a program for collecting donations to people in need. Discuss with the young people the scope of the program and the recipients of the donations. Decide together how to distribute the coupons and where the donated items will go.

4. If you have more than twelve participants, divide them into small groups. Distribute paper, pens or pencils, and black markers. Invite each group to create a rough draft of at least two different designs for a Christian coupon that includes the message "Buy two food items, give one away." Each design should be similar in dimension and style to an authentic grocery store coupon. It might also incorporate an appropriate scriptural verse, and it should state the date by which the donations must be delivered, the place where the donations are to be taken, and the name of the agency that will eventually receive the food.

5.   When the designs are complete, invite everyone to select one idea from among the rough drafts. Ask for one or two people to create the final coupon based on the winning design. Before the next gathering, make multiple copies of the coupon on card stock. You may want to create a flyer to distribute with the coupons, explaining the program and describing the agency that will receive the donated items.

6.   At the subsequent gathering, give each young person a number of coupons and decide where the participants will distribute them. The young people might give out the coupons at church and at parish events. With the permission of store managers, they might even distribute the coupons at shopping malls and grocery stores.

7.   After the donated items have been collected, gather the young people to deliver the food to the designated agency or groups. That will give the young teens a personal connection with those whom they are serving.

8.   Close by making the young people aware of the Gospel call to simplicity and the importance of that message, which is counter to most of the messages in the media culture of our time. Affirm their efforts to encourage others to think twice about what they buy and how they spend their money. Note that through this activity, they have spread the message that for people in need to live, everyone must strive to share resources with them.

ALTERNATIVE APPROACHES

- ◎ Begin this activity with the "Commercial Sing-Off" strategy found on pages 38–40 of this manual.
- ◎ This activity works well as a seasonal project for Lent, spring break, summer, or Thanksgiving.
- ◎ The coupons may be placed at the entrances to the church, with a poster explaining the project and a box or basket in which donations can be placed.
- ◎ The coupons do not have to be for food. Instead they could be for clothing or for household items, depending on the needs of the recipients. For example, you might create coupons for jeans, socks, toothpaste, winter hats and mittens, baby clothing, kitchen utensils, or bedding.
- ◎ At the distribution meeting, invite the recipients, or workers or residents of the recipient program, to bless the gifts that have been donated.

SCRIPTURAL CONNECTIONS

◎ Luke 6:38 (Give, and it will be given you.)
◎ Acts 20:35 (It is more blessed to give than to receive.)
◎ 2 Cor. 9:7 (God loves a cheerful giver.)
◎ James 1:17 (Every good and perfect gift is from God.)

NOTES

Use the space below to jot notes and reminders for the next time you use this strategy.

Commercial Sing-Off

This strategy challenges groups of the young teens to out-sing one another and test their knowledge of commercial jingles. It is an ideal activity to accompany a meeting or service activity that focuses on commercialism or the culture of consumerism.

Suggested Time

10 to 20 minutes

Group Size

This activity works best as a contest between at least four teams, with five to ten people on each team. However, it can also work with a small group divided into pairs.

Materials Needed

- newsprint and markers
- a coin (optional)

PROCEDURE

Preparation. It might be helpful to recruit another adult to serve as the adjudicator for the sing-off. Or, if your group is large, you might appoint a panel of young teens to fill that role.

1. The young people may view commercials as simply entertainment. To challenge that notion, begin with a brief comment about commercialism's effects on people. Invite the young teens to reflect on their exposure to marketing influences that have enabled them to internalize a vast number of commercial messages.

2. Divide the group into approximately four teams of at least two people (preferably five to ten people). Give each team a sheet of newsprint and a marker. Direct each team to elect one person to take notes and another person to be its lead singer.

Send the teams to the far corners of the room. Announce that they each have 5 minutes to come up with a list of musical jingles from radio or television commercials. Explain that they will perform those jingles in a competition, and they should list as many as possible in the time allotted.

3. When the teams have completed their lists, outline the following rules for the competition:

The teams will take turns singing the songs they have identified.

When it is a team's turn, its lead singer chooses one of the jingles listed by the team and starts the team singing the jingle.

A team is eliminated from the competition when any of the following things occurs:

The song it sings is not recognized by me or an adjudicator.

It repeats a jingle that another team has already sung.

It is unable to start a new jingle on cue from the lead singer.

It runs out of commercial songs.

When the allotted time is up, the team with the longest remaining list of jingles wins. If all but one team fold before the time is up, the remaining team is the winner.

4. Direct the young people to stand in their teams and face off in the center of the room. Toss a coin or use another arbitrary method to determine the starting team. Encourage the teams to sing their commercial choices as loudly as possible, and moderate their activity until time expires or all but one team are eliminated.

5. To conclude the activity, choose a few jingles and ask the participants to explain the messages they communicate. Comment on the subtle influences of commercialism, noting how many jingles the young people were able to come up with in a short amount of time and how well they knew the lyrics. Challenge them to filter commercial messages through what they know about basic human needs versus luxuries and desires, and to make wise decisions about what they purchase or ask for. Encourage them to open their ears and eyes to the message that comes from God.

ALTERNATIVE APPROACHES

◎ To provide a contrast between the influences of commercial culture and the influences of the Gospels, immediately following the commercial sing-off, invite the young people to share their knowledge of the most famous words of Jesus. Challenge the teams to complete some well-known scriptural quotes, such as "Blessed are the meek . . ." (Matt. 5:5, NRSV) and "Wherever your treasure is . . ." (Matt. 6:21, NJB).

◎ Challenge each team to create a musical jingle that has a Gospel message.

◎ Record commercials from the radio or television and invite the group to analyze and discuss the message, techniques, and values promoted in each advertisement.

◎ Conclude with a prayer service that inspires the young teens to look for messages that are not often found in commercial culture—messages of hope, peace, service, and justice.

SCRIPTURAL CONNECTIONS

◎ Isa. 6:8–10 (Here I am, Lord.)

◎ Matt. 6:25–34 (Do not worry about your life and what you are to eat or wear.)

◎ Matt. 13:3–23 (The parable of the sower and the seed)

◎ 1 Cor. 13:8–13 (In the end three things will last: faith, hope, and love.)

NOTES

Use the space below to jot notes and reminders for the next time you use this strategy.

The Cost of Living

This hands-on activity raises awareness of the complex systems of injustice behind a global economic market. It offers the young teens an opportunity to get personal about their role as consumers and the value they place on comfort and appearance. It also invites them to reflect on some of the contrasting realities of life that are a result of our system of commerce.

Suggested Time

About 60 minutes

Group Size

This strategy can be done with a group of from four to about sixty people.

Materials Needed

- ☼ a candle
- ☼ a Bible
- ☼ paper
- ☼ pens or pencils
- ☼ labels or small price tags, four for each person
- ☼ calculators (optional)
- ☼ a scissors
- ☼ poster board
- ☼ a hole punch
- ☼ string or yarn
- ☼ glue sticks or rolls of cellophane tape, one for every four to seven people

:¤: markers, one for every four to seven people
:¤: one copy of resource 1, "The Price of Life"
:¤: one copy of resource 2, "The Words of Life"

PROCEDURE

Preparation. Cut large price tags from poster board. Punch a hole in each tag and attach a piece of string or yarn through the hole. You will need one price tag for every four to seven young people.

Cut into individual strips the facts on resource 1 and the quotes on resource 2. Keep the two sets separate.

Create a prayer space by placing together a candle, a Bible that is opened to Luke 12:13–34, paper, pens or pencils, calculators if you have them available, markers, and the strips you have cut from resources 1 and 2.

1. Begin with a brief prayer service. Light a candle and read Luke 12:13–34. Encourage the young people to reflect on the passage's meaning and message for them.

2. Lead a discussion around the following questions:

When was the last time you went to a mall or another shopping center?

What did you buy, and how much did you spend?

What was the most recent thing you bought for yourself?

If you were given a fifty-dollar coupon for your favorite store, what would you do with it?

What is one thing that you need or would like to have right now, something you have been asking your parents to buy for you?

3. Divide the participants into groups of four to seven people. Direct each team to choose an "accountant." Give each accountant one sheet of paper for each person in the group, a pen or pencil for each person, and enough labels or small price tags so that each person in the group gets four. Tell the accountants to distribute the items to their group members. You may also want to distribute calculators among the groups.

4. Direct the young people each to place a label or price tag on four items they are wearing or have in their possession. To ensure variety encourage them to work with the other people in their group to choose different items for each person.

When each person has tagged four items, instruct the groups to estimate the purchase price of each item and mark the label or price tag. Direct everyone to tally their own total for their four items. Then ask the group accountants each to add together all the individual totals in their group to come up with the overall purchase value for their group.

Ask the accountants each to share their group's total with everyone. Compare the final tallies. Name the group with the highest total the MVG (Most Valuable Group).

5. Lead the participants in a discussion of the following questions:

What is your most prized possession?

Is there one thing that you have set your heart on buying?

Do you know any wealthy people?

Do you consider yourself to be a wealthy person? Would others consider you wealthy?

Who are the most valuable people to you? Why?

Does wealth make one person more important than another?

Remind the young people about the reading from Luke's Gospel that they heard during the opening prayer. Then continue with the following questions:

Why did Jesus command us to live simply?

Do you find it hard to live simply in our culture? Why or why not?

Is it wrong for people to have more than they need?

6. Distribute one oversized price tag, a glue stick or roll of cellophane tape, and a marker to each group. Invite the groups each to select one price-of-life fact (from resource 1) and one words-of-life quote (from resource 2) for their oversized tag. Direct them to glue or tape the fact and quote to the oversized tag; label the oversized tag with the brand name, "The Price of Life"; and attach each member's personal labels or price tags to the oversized tag.

7. Invite someone from each group to read the group's fact and quote to everyone. Comment on the facts and the quotes, noting the basic truth that all people are worthy of life. Explain that to make that truth real, we must be aware of two things:

Everyone shares the responsibility in a system that values life according to material wealth.

When we understand the implications of our choices, we can make decisions based on a different standard and set of values, putting the holiness of life and the sanctity of human relationships and community over material goods.

Challenge the young teens to imagine a world in which the things that our culture often overvalues (possessions, money, influence, and celebrity status) are reduced in price, and the things that are often undervalued (human life, family, relationships, community, and the earth's resources) are made precious.

8. Invite someone from each group to put the group's Price of Life tag near the Bible and candle in the prayer space. Close with a prayer that encourages the young teens to affirm one thing they will do to live more simply and share with those who are needy.

ALTERNATIVE APPROACHES

- To take the price tag symbol further, make a single large tag and attach to it all the scriptural quotes and facts. The young people may decorate this tag with their own logo. Hang the tag on a large crucifix as a symbol of the sacrifice that impoverished people must make in order to live.
- Encourage the young teens and their families to reduce and simplify by taking blank tags home, tagging items that are not being used, and delivering those items to a donation center.
- The Price of Life tags may be made by young teens for the whole parish, to promote a drive for items such as blankets, food, or furniture for needy people or social programs.

NOTES

Use the space below to jot notes and reminders for the next time you use this strategy.

The Price of Life

At least 700 million people in the world are severely undernourished because they cannot afford to meet their basic nutritional needs (*Operation Rice Bowl Lenten Program*).

In our human family of six billion people, one billion are forced to live every day with unsafe drinking water and without proper sanitation (*Operation Rice Bowl Lenten Program*).

One in every six people on our planet lives on less than one dollar a day. More than 1.2 billion people spend their entire life in absolute poverty (*Operation Rice Bowl Lenten Program*).

In 1996 U.S. citizens spent one hundred times more on entertainment and recreation than their government spent on food programs for poor women and children (*Catholic Social Teaching and Human Rights,* page F-3).

Almost thirty-five million people suffer hunger and malnutrition in the United States (*Catholic Social Teaching and Human Rights,* page F-3).

The 225 richest people in the world receive 50 percent of the world's total income; the 1.25 billion poorest people in the world receive only 1.1 percent of the world's total income (*Celebrate Jubilee and Justice!*).

In 1996 in the United States, 14.5 million children (people under eighteen years old) were living below the federal poverty line (*Catholic Social Teaching and Human Rights,* page C-6).

Since 1969 child poverty rates have risen by one-half while the nation's economic wealth has doubled (*Catholic Social Teaching and Human Rights,* page C-6).

One-half of all children's deaths around the world are related to hunger (*Catholic Social Teaching and Human Rights,* page F-3).

It is estimated that eighteen million people in our world die each year from hunger-related causes (*Catholic Social Teaching and Human Rights,* page C-6).

The Words of Life

Do not store treasure for yourself on earth. Store your treasure in heaven, for where your treasure is, there will your heart be. (Adapted from Matthew 6:19–21)

Set your hearts first on God's Reign and on God's saving justice, and all else will be given you. (Adapted from Matthew 6:33)

If you want to be perfect, sell your possessions and give to the poor. It is hard for a rich person to enter heaven. (Adapted from Matthew 19:21–23)

The worries of the world and the lure of riches choke the word. (Adapted from Mark 4:19)

Blessed are you who are poor; the Reign of God is yours. But woe to you who are rich; you have already had your reward. (Adapted from Luke 6:20–24)

No one can serve two masters. You cannot serve both God and money. (Adapted from Luke 16:13)

The Son has come to seek out and save what is lost. (Adapted from Luke 19:10)

The love of money is the root of all evil, and in their eagerness to be rich, some people have wandered away from the faith. (Adapted from 1 Timothy 6:10)

Warn those rich in goods not to be proud or look down on others. (Adapted from 1 Timothy 6:17)

Come now, you rich people, weep for the miseries that will come to you. (Adapted from James 5:1)

Good Sam Guide:
A Hometown
Survival Manual
for Life in the Streets

This project gives the young teens the opportunity to provide a valuable resource for needy people while also learning about the realities of poverty and local support services for those who are poor.

Suggested Time

The preparation, reflection, and division of tasks may require 45 to 60 minutes. The research will likely take several weeks or more. This project could even be adopted as a summerlong service activity.

Group Size

This project will work for any size group, as long as enough adults are available to assist the young people.

Special Considerations

This project requires research into community services and involves making connections with professional service agencies. Recruit additional adults to help you and the young people complete the necessary tasks; you will need one adult for each of five small groups of young people. The Good Sam Guide can be as simple or as creative and exhaustive as your time and energy permit.

Materials Needed

- ☼ a tape or CD player, and a recording of reflective music (optional)
- ☼ a pillar candle and matches
- ☼ a Bible
- ☼ newsprint and markers
- ☼ masking tape
- ☼ local phone books, diocesan directories, newspapers, and other sources of information about services to poor and needy people

PROCEDURE

Preparation. Read the guided reflection in procedure step 2. If necessary adapt it so that it is more applicable to your community.

Write each of the following headings at the top of a separate sheet of newsprint:

- ◎ I was homeless.
- ◎ I was hungry and thirsty.
- ◎ I was naked, cold, and ashamed.
- ◎ I was sick.
- ◎ I was a stranger, lost and alone.

Post the sheets in the meeting place.

Familiarize yourself with the social-service agencies, shelters, community kitchens, and food pantries in the vicinity of the parish or school.

1. Ask the young people to be still and listen carefully to the words of the Scriptures. If you are using reflective music, begin playing it at this time. Light a candle, then slowly read Matt. 25:34–40.

2. Invite the young people to close their eyes and enter into the following scenario. Read the reflection, stopping for a few seconds at each ellipses.

Imagine that you are a stranger in this town. . . . You have just arrived in this neighborhood. . . . How far did you have to walk to get here? Were you dropped downtown by a bus or a train? . . .

The place is unfamiliar to you, and you know no one. . . . Does it seems like a welcoming place for a stranger? . . .

Imagine that you are penniless. You have no money. . . . Why are you here? . . . Are you lost? . . . Are you ill? Do you need medication or medical treatment? . . . Have you run away from home? . . . Are you struggling with an addiction or mental illness? . . . Do you have your children or other family members with you? . . .

You are a stranger—hungry, lost, penniless, and unknown in a strange place. . . . Where will you go for help? . . . for a place to stay? . . . for something to eat? . . . for a shower and some clean clothes? . . .

for medical help? . . . Where will you go to meet someone who will notice you, listen to you, and offer to help?

Imagine now that it is not you but Jesus who has walked into this neighborhood as a stranger—homeless, lost, penniless, and alone. . . . How is he received? . . . Where does he go to find help?

3. Lead the group in a discussion of the following questions:

Have you noticed lost, hungry, homeless people in your community?

Where might you see strangers or homeless people in your community?

Where do they go for help? Who helps them?

Are they your neighbors?

How can you help them?

4. Point out the newsprint sheets that you prepared and posted before the session. Brainstorm with the whole group the kinds of people who are most likely to fit under each heading. For example, the list under "I was homeless" could include immigrants, refugees, illegal aliens, migrant workers, street people, families that have no work, residents of nursing homes or public institutions, and runaway teenagers.

5. Read Luke 10:30–37. Discuss with the young people how Jesus responded to the question, "Who is my neighbor?" by telling the story of a foreigner who was identified as a true neighbor because he stopped to notice a person who was hurt and found the right place for him.

Invite the group to respond to Jesus' challenge by creating a Good Sam Guide—an informative guide for strangers or homeless people that can be copied and distributed around the community.

6. Divide the young people into five small groups, each with an adult facilitator. Give each group one of the newsprint lists, a blank sheet of newsprint, and some markers. Distribute local phone books, diocesan directories, newspapers, and other resources among the groups. Some places that the groups may want to include in the Good Sam Guide are as follows:
◎ churches
◎ emergency shelters and day centers for street people
◎ the nearest clinic, hospital, and emergency room
◎ designated safe places (marked by a special sign) for children and teens
◎ feeding programs and food pantries
◎ thrift shops and consignment stores
◎ meeting places for Alcoholics Anonymous, Narcotics Anonymous, Gamblers Anonymous, and so forth

- Saint Vincent de Paul stores and centers
- the Salvation Army
- Volunteers of America
- long-term shelter programs for adults, families, and teens
- a Catholic Worker community house of hospitality
- church-sponsored social service agencies, such as Catholic Charities

Encourage the participants to include the important information that a stranger in a difficult situation would need to know about the community and the neighborhood. They should provide the exact name of each agency, its address, and its phone number, as well as other pertinent information such as when meals are served or when the business or office is open.

Some of this information may be readily available, and some may require research. In any case tell the young people to make a personal connection with each agency before listing it in the Good Sam Guide. Ask the adult in each group to coordinate the research and contact efforts. Establish a deadline for returning with information, and set a target date for the completion and distribution of the manual.

7. Discuss with the young people the format of the Good Sam Guide. Possibilities are a one-page flyer, a double-sided card, a trifold leaflet, a simple booklet, and a poster. Include a simple map of the neighborhood or community as part of the guide.

Also discuss the most useful locations for distributing copies of the Good Sam Guide. They might be placed with local store owners, at bus and train stations, on notice boards, in the vestibules of local churches, with church staff members, with parishioners, with families of young people, and so on.

8. Arrange for someone to create the final product. Depending on the format, one or two young teens may have the technical expertise to create a master copy on a home computer. You might want to ask a printer to donate copies, or ask area businesses to contribute to the cost of the layout and printing.

Also decide as a group where to distribute the guide, and then make the necessary arrangements. For example, if the group wants to make the guide available at a local supermarket, contact the store owner or manager.

9. To conclude the project, send the young people out in groups with adults to distribute copies of the Good Sam Guide to the prearranged locations. Encourage the groups to stop and offer a prayer or blessing at each place they visit.

ALTERNATIVE APPROACHES

◎ Invite other churches and social agencies to participate in the project. This might be an activity for several church youth groups to work on together.

◎ Involve the local news media—especially the local Catholic newspaper—in the Good Sam Guide project by inviting the young teens to write and send out brief press reports. Be sure to arrange for an adult to supervise the efforts.

◎ Instead of compiling one guide, create several small guides, each focusing on one specific area of need. In this way the group could either limit the scope of the project, or stagger the project by creating new guides at different points throughout the year.

◎ As part of the development process, ask the young people to compose a good Samaritan prayer of blessing for all those in need. Include the prayer in the guide.

SCRIPTURAL CONNECTIONS

◎ Lev. 25:35 (Look after the poor as you do a stranger.)

◎ Ps. 146:9 (God protects strangers.)

◎ Isa. 58:7 (Share bread, provide shelter, and clothe the naked.)

◎ Matt. 5:40 (If someone asks for your tunic, give your cloak also.)

◎ Heb. 13:2 (Provide hospitality to strangers, and you may entertain angels along the way.)

◎ James 2:14–18 (Faith must be accompanied by good deeds.)

NOTES

Use the space below to jot notes and reminders for the next time you use this strategy.

Join the Dots

OVERVIEW

This icebreaker helps the young people make the connection between belonging and the kind of exclusion that lies at the root of racism. Simple directions and colored dots invite the participants to form their own small groups that both include and exclude.

Suggested Time

5 to 10 minutes

Group Size

This activity works best with groups of twenty or more young people. If your group is smaller than twenty, adapt the exercise by reducing the variety and number of colored dots.

Materials Needed

- ☼ adhesive labels or name tags, one for each person
- ☼ markers in seven different colors

PROCEDURE

Preparation. Draw a dot in the middle of each of three labels or name tags, using a different colored marker for each dot. Set those three labels or tags aside. Then divide the remaining labels or tags into four approximately equal sets. Choose a different colored marker for each of the remaining four sets, and use it to draw a dot in the middle of each label or tag in the set. You should end up with seven sets of labels or tags, marked with dots in seven different colors—for example, if you have twenty-two participants, you might have one label with a yellow dot, one with blue, one with red, five with green, five with purple, five with orange, and four with black.

1. Ask the participants to close their eyes and remain quiet. Move around the group, sticking a label or tag on the front of each person's shirt until everyone has a label or tag with a colored dot. Be sure that the various colors are spread throughout the group.

2. Without mentioning the colored dots and keeping the instructions deliberately brief, tell the young people to open their eyes, move around the room, and find their own group. They must remain silent until everyone is in the right group.

3. When the young people have formed their groups, ask them to sit with those groups. Lead a discussion around the following questions:

What were you asked to do for this activity? What happened?

Did people assume that they had to fall into groups according to the colored dots?

What happened to those who did not have a color group?

If you were in a color group, why did you or did you not invite the people who were not part of a color group into your group?

4. If the young people formed groups according to colored dots without being told to do so, conclude the activity by making the following comments in your own words:

Just as you had no real basis for forming groups according to an external color marker, in real life people have no real basis for excluding people or groups because of race.

People often develop associations, make judgments, and form opinions of others based solely on externals like clothes, body shape, skin color, and appearance.

As Christians we are called to look deeper into people and see who they *really* are rather than making judgments about them based on false criteria. That process takes time and requires that we look and listen with our heart.

ALTERNATIVE APPROACHES

- After the groups have formed once, challenge them to re-form in silence so that each group represents a diversity of color.
- If time permits, invite the young people to deepen the discussion by sharing information about the other groups they belong to. The following questions may be helpful:
  - What groups do you belong to?
  - How would you describe the group you usually spend time with at school? Who is in and who is out?
  - How do you know when you are in the "right" group?
- Invite the participants to create a colorful visual image in the form of a connect-the-dots puzzle. With markers or stickers, they should use dots to outline the words of a simple phrase, then number the dots. The message can be read only when the numbered dots are joined together. Suggested phrases are the following: "We all belong together," "One God and one family," and "Many colors make a better picture."

SCRIPTURAL CONNECTIONS

- Deut. 10:17–19 (Love those who are not part of your group, because you were also not part of a group.)
- Matt. 10:40 (Whoever welcomes another person welcomes Jesus.)
- Matt. 25:35 (I was a stranger, and you made me feel welcome.)
- Rom. 15:7 (Accept one another, for the sake of God's glory.)

NOTES

Use the space below to jot notes and reminders for the next time you use this strategy.

(This strategy is adapted from Christian Aid, "Coloured Dot Game.")

Mercy Works:
The Hands-on Gospel

OVERVIEW

This activity uses a hand motif to make a connection with the corporal works of mercy as listed in Matthew's Gospel. The young teens are challenged to find ways to practice each of those Christian actions. A tangible end result, a wreath of hands, serves as a visible symbol of the acts of service performed by the young people.

Suggested Time

About 20 minutes to explain the project and create the hand shapes. The participants may perform the five works of mercy over a period of several weeks or months.

Group Size

This strategy can be done with any size group.

Materials Needed

- ☼ a Bible
- ☼ newsprint and markers
- ☼ colored construction paper
- ☼ pens or pencils
- ☼ scissors
- ☼ glue sticks, tape, or a stapler
- ☼ copies of resource 3, "Works of Mercy," one for every two people

☼ poster board
☼ a candle and matches

PROCEDURE

Preparation. Copy resource 3 on colored paper. Each copy will give you two sets of the works of mercy; be sure you have one set for each person in your group. Cut apart the strips as scored and put them into six stacks, one stack for each work. Place the stacks facedown on the floor or a tabletop.

1. Recruit a volunteer to read Matt. 25:31–46. Ask the group to identify the six practices of Christianity—also called works of mercy—that are named in the passage. List those on newsprint, and invite the young people to share how they have used their hands to practice one or more of those mercy works. Encourage them to move beyond a literal interpretation of the passage and look for a broader application of each work. For example, visiting a prisoner could be interpreted as spending time with someone who is a shut-in or who is struggling with loneliness. Giving food or drink could also imply offering friendship to someone who is outcast, as could learning the name of someone who is homeless or listening to their story.

Note: The Scripture passage from Matthew lists six of the seven corporal works of mercy. The seventh is Bury the dead. It is not necessary to discuss that mercy work in this activity, or to identify the corporal works of mercy as distinguished from the spiritual works of mercy. However, you should be prepared to address questions about those other works of mercy if they arise. See *Catechism of the Catholic Church,* by the Libreria Editrice Vaticana, translated by the United States Catholic Conference (USCC) (Washington, DC: USCC, 1994), number 2447, for background on the works of mercy.

2. Distribute a sheet of colored paper to each person and make pens or pencils, markers, scissors, and glue sticks, tape, or a stapler available to the group. Direct the young people each to draw around one of their hands, cut out the shape, and write their name and the phrase, "Hand of God," on the palm.

3. Point out the stacks of paper slips from resource 3 that you prepared before the meeting. Tell the young people that each stack represents one of the six mercy works listed on the newsprint. Each person is to select randomly five works and glue each work to the back of one of the fingers on their hand cutout so that it can be read.

4. After the young people have attached five works of mercy to their hand, ask them to think about which of those acts they have already accomplished and write a two- or three-word description of each act on the inside (palm side) of the corresponding finger on their hand cutout. When they finish writing, direct them to curl each finger slightly toward the palm so that the hand forms a gesture of giving or receiving.

5. On poster board make a wreath by gluing, taping, or stapling the young people's hand shapes in a circle with the fingers pointing to the outside. In the center of the circle, write, "The Hands-on gospel according to [name or description of the group]." Place the wreath in a prominent place in the parish or school.

6. Encourage the young people to perform additional works of mercy, particularly any they have not already done. Set a time limit for this process. At subsequent gatherings take the wreath down and ask the young people to write on the appropriate fingers of their paper hand, descriptions of the mercy works they have completed since the last meeting. Replace the wreath in its original position after each update.

7. At the conclusion of the time allotted for adding to the wreath, gather the group around the wreath. Light a candle and read Luke 6:30–36. Invite the participants to mention in prayer the names of those who have taught them how to be merciful.

ALTERNATIVE APPROACHES

- The hand idea can be extended to include a second wreath for the spiritual works of mercy. Direct the young people to write the five key verbs from the seven spiritual works of mercy (comfort, counsel, pray, forgive, and teach) on the fingers of a second hand cutout and add concrete examples of things they have done in those areas. Refer to the *Catechism,* number 2447, for background on the spiritual works of mercy.
- Make copies of the participants' finished works-of-mercy hands, front and back, and place them inside the parish or school bulletin or youth newsletter. Or send the copies home for the young people's families as a Lenten or Advent project, and encourage the families to make their own wreath.
- Invite parents and sponsors of Confirmation candidates to contribute their hands to the wreath.
- Hang the wreath in the youth room, classroom, or church gathering area and attach pictures from outreach activities to form a display or mobile.
- Include the wreath in the offertory procession at a stewardship or service day liturgy or as part of a Confirmation liturgy.

SCRIPTURAL CONNECTIONS

- Matt. 5:7 (Happy are those who are merciful to others; God will be merciful to them.)
- Rom. 12:6–13 (In all things and to all people, do good.)
- 2 Cor. 9:7 (God loves the one who gives gladly.)
- Eph. 4:32 (Be kind, tenderhearted, and forgiving.)
- Col. 3:12 (Clothe yourselves with compassion, kindness, humility, gentleness, and patience.)

NOTES

Use the space below to jot notes and reminders for the next time you use this strategy.

Works of Mercy

Feed the Hungry
I am often hungry, undernourished, and in need of food, friendship, and company. Will you stop, notice me, and feed me?

Give Drink to the Thirsty
I am thirsty, in need of something or someone to revive me and give me hope. I need justice and fairness and someone to notice me. Will you stop and listen to me?

Clothe the Naked
I am cold, exposed, and vulnerable, without proper clothing and adequate housing. I need human warmth, a place to belong, and someone who cares about me. Will you stop and notice and show that you care for me?

Welcome the Stranger
I am a stranger in a new school, a strange town, a foreign country. I am an exile, a refugee. I know no one, have no relatives or friends, and need someone to trust. Will you pay attention to me and give me a chance?

Visit the Prisoner
I am locked away, cut off and discarded from society. I need friendship and someone to be concerned about me. I want to be treated with respect and dignity. Will you give some time to me and take the risk of knowing me?

Visit the Sick
I am ill, often in pain and weak. I am isolated and frustrated and long to be healthy again. Will you come to see me? Will you help me pass the hours, let me share my fears, and help me to laugh?

Feed the Hungry
I am often hungry, undernourished, and in need of food, friendship, and company. Will you stop, notice me, and feed me?

Give Drink to the Thirsty
I am thirsty, in need of something or someone to revive me and give me hope. I need justice and fairness and someone to notice me. Will you stop and listen to me?

Clothe the Naked
I am cold, exposed, and vulnerable, without proper clothing and adequate housing. I need human warmth, a place to belong, and someone who cares about me. Will you stop and notice and show that you care for me?

Welcome the Stranger
I am a stranger in a new school, a strange town, a foreign country. I am an exile, a refugee. I know no one, have no relatives or friends, and need someone to trust. Will you pay attention to me and give me a chance?

Visit the Prisoner
I am locked away, cut off and discarded from society. I need friendship and someone to be concerned about me. I want to be treated with respect and dignity. Will you give some time to me and take the risk of knowing me?

Visit the Sick
I am ill, often in pain and weak. I am isolated and frustrated and long to be healthy again. Will you come to see me? Will you help me pass the hours, let me share my fears, and help me to laugh?

The Eyes Have It

This simulation challenges the young people to look at the human tendencies to compete, judge others, and create divisions between people. It carries a clear message about the deep-seated roots of prejudice in human nature.

Suggested Time

10 to 15 minutes

Group Size

This strategy can be done with any size group.

Materials Needed

- ☼ one copy of resource 4, "Light Eyes, Dim Wits?"
- ☼ a recent newspaper or news magazine (optional)
- ☼ a Bible
- ☼ a small mirror

PROCEDURE

Preparation. You may want to paste a copy of resource 4 into a recent newspaper or news magazine so that it will appear that you are reading the article from an authentic source.

1. Nonchalantly ask if anyone read the recent article in (name a newspaper or magazine), about how intelligence is connected with eye color. Read the article from resource 4.

2. Be sure that the young people understand the implications and assertions of the article. Invite them to respond to what they heard, and ask clarifying questions. Observe the responses of various groups and individuals who challenge the information, those who endorse it, those who celebrate it as an affirmation of their own intelligence, and those who recognize it as a hoax.

3. Inform the young people that the article was a ruse intended to uncover the hidden tendency we all have to judge, compare, and be swayed by the judgments of others. Encourage them to share the feelings they had when they understood the message contained in the article. Ask if it makes any more sense to judge and categorize people according to hair color, skin color, weight, ethnic group, or gender.

If time permits invite the young people to discuss their personal experiences of feeling excluded or judged because of their appearance, age, gender, ethnic group, or religious beliefs. Also invite them to talk about—or at least think about—situations in which they have excluded or demeaned others.

Consider pointing out that we may be less quick to judge others if we think about what we read and hear, and question information that seems prejudicial or biased or simply suspicious.

4. Gather the young people in a circle. Conclude the activity by reading 1 Sam. 16:7. Pass around a small mirror and invite each person to take a silent moment to look deeply into his or her own eyes. In the silence invite everyone to pray for eyes that see others as God sees them. Close by commenting that when we take the risk of looking into our own eyes or the eyes of another person, we are looking into a soul. And only then can we see as God sees.

ALTERNATIVE APPROACHES

⊚ Begin the activity by blindfolding the first three participants that arrive. Challenge the rest of the group to guess the eye color of the mystery young teens. Ask them to explain the criteria they used when they were guessing. Then read the article and continue the activity as described in the Procedure section.

◎ Invite the young people (individually or in small groups) to write a brief poem, devise a skit, or create a poster or slogan that responds to the question, Why did God gift us with eyes of different colors?

◎ Pass around variously colored transparent plastic sheets, sunglasses, or lenses, and invite the participants to describe how they see the world differently through the assorted lenses. Discuss the range of influences that can color the way we view the world, such as culture, upbringing, values and belief system, personal experiences, and education. Conclude by remarking that we each perceive reality differently, and what we believe about life and our world determines how and what we see.

◎ If time permits close the activity by reading the complete story of the call of David the teenager in 1 Sam. 16:1–13.

SCRIPTURAL CONNECTIONS

◎ Matt. 13:14 (They will look and look but not see.)

◎ Luke 11:34–36 (The eyes are like a lamp for the body.)

◎ John 9:39 (Jesus came so that the blind would see and the sighted would become blind.)

◎ John 20:24–29 (Happy are those who believe without seeing.)

NOTES

Use the space below to jot notes and reminders for the next time you use this strategy.

Light Eyes, Dim Wits?

A team of eminent biologists and psychologists working as part of a ten-year federal study has concluded that human intelligence can be correlated with eye color. According to leading psychologist Dr. R. A. Cyst, "The color of the human eye can be connected with the level of intelligence a human being can attain."

Dr. Cyst's team has developed a system for the measurement of human intelligence based on the theory that darker eye colors absorb more light and offer greater stimulation to the human brain. According to the study, individuals with black or dark brown pigmentation in their eyes have a greater intelligence potential than those with light brown, green, or blue coloration. People with light blue eyes (which absorb the least amount of light), it has been concluded, have the lowest potential for acquiring intelligence. In an interview for a national news program, Dr. Cyst added: "No amount of schooling can offset defective light eye coloring. The sad fact is that baby blues inevitably mean dim wits."

Resource 4: Permission to reproduce this resource for program use is granted.

63

The Narrow Door: A Guided Meditation

OVERVIEW

In their mind's eye, the young teens investigate the closets of their own bedroom, gather their possessions, and carry those belongings through a series of narrow doors. This guided meditation communicates the Gospel message of simple living in a way that engages the imagination and inspires the young people to actively simplify their lives.

Suggested Time

30 to 45 minutes

Group Size

Given adequate space and a proper environment, this strategy can be done with any size group.

Special Considerations

As a prayer technique, guided meditation requires specific attention to the environment. Above all, the participants need to be encouraged to relax and focus, avoiding any disturbance or distraction. Ideally, the young people should be able to lie on a carpeted floor with their head on a pillow or cushion. In a classroom setting, they may put their head on their desk. It also helps to light a candle, dim the lights, and use quiet background music.

Materials Needed

- ☼ candles and matches
- ☼ pillows, one for each person (optional)
- ☼ a tape or CD player, and a recording of reflective music (optional)
- ☼ one copy of resource 5, "The Narrow Door"
- ☼ a flashlight (optional)
- ☼ a blanket or sheet

PROCEDURE

1. Light a candle and dim the lights in the meeting room. If possible gather the young people in a circle and ask them to lie on their back with their head facing in to the center of the circle. Provide a pillow for each person if you can. Be sure that the participants leave adequate space between themselves and the next person so that distractions will be minimized. Tell them that they will be experiencing a form of prayer that uses their imagination.

If you have reflective music available, begin playing it at this time. Request silence and invite the young people to close their eyes, listen to the music, and become aware of their own breathing. When they are silent, invite them to listen closely to your voice as you read them a meditation.

2. Read the meditation from resource 5. If the room is dark, you may need another candle or a small flashlight.

3. After the meditation lead the young people back to the present moment by inviting them to listen to their breathing once again, be aware of the sounds around them, and slowly open their eyes. Ask them to sit up and gather their thoughts. Use the following questions as guides to engage them in a brief discussion of the experience and implications of the meditation:

How well were you able to envision your room and all the things that you keep there?

Were you surprised, or shocked, at the amount of stuff in your room, or were you already aware of how much you have?

What were some of the items that you were able to carry out of your room?

What were some of the most precious things that you did not want to part with?

Which of the four doors was most difficult for you to pass through?

How might the words of Jesus apply to your life right now?

How can you begin to live more simply right now?

What do you have to do to unburden yourself and become more available to God and God's people?

4. Place a blanket or sheet on the floor and invite people to carefully place on it one item they have with them, such as a purse, pencil, key, ring, watch, or cap. Note that these items are symbols of the belongings we use every day as well as of larger possessions—such as jewelry and property—that many people spend their lives acquiring and protecting.

Read Luke 18:24–25. Reflect with the group on how Jesus addressed those words to a young man who was unable or unwilling to follow Jesus because of his attachment to possessions. Invite the young people to share a prayer for the gift to live lighter and let go of the desire for unnecessary material things.

ALTERNATIVE APPROACHES

◉ Instead of asking the young people to place personal things on a blanket or sheet, set up a display on a blanket or sheet yourself. Include symbols such as these:

- ◉ a watch, symbolic of the wealth of time that can be shared or hoarded
- ◉ a gold chain, symbolic of how wealth and possessions can imprison us
- ◉ a candy bar, symbolic of the excesses of eating and dieting
- ◉ a wallet, symbolic of the energy dedicated to the acquisition of wealth
- ◉ a music CD, symbolic of creativity that is put at the service of consumption
- ◉ a baseball cap, symbolic of the commercial image of sports entertainment
- ◉ a popular magazine, symbolic of the influences of advertising

Include any other articles that symbolize the pressures and influences that complicate the lives of young adolescents. In closing the activity, invite the young people to take one object they feel drawn to and share why they chose it and what it symbolizes for them. Then ask each person to return their chosen object and share a prayer or a commitment to living more simply.

◉ Send the message from this activity home by directing the young people each to make a recipe-for-simplicity card. Give everyone an index card and direct them to copy the following quotations on one side of it:

- ◉ "When someone steals another's clothes, we call them a thief. Should we not give the same name to one who could clothe the naked and does not?" (Saint Basil the Great).
- ◉ "The bread in your cupboard belongs to the hungry; the coat hanging unused in your closet belongs to the one who needs it; the shoes rotting in your closet belong to the one who has no shoes; the money which you hoard up belongs to the poor"(Saint Basil the Great).
- ◉ "Give to everyone who asks you, and do not ask for your property back from someone who takes it. Treat others as you would like people to treat you" (Luke 6:30–31, NJB).

Direct them to write on the opposite side of the card the heading, "A home-style recipe for simple living," and list the numbers 1 to 6. Tell them to take their card home and ask their family to commit to six concrete ways to live more simply. Encourage them to bring their family's ideas to the next meeting.

SCRIPTURAL CONNECTIONS

◉ Matt. 11:28–30 (Come to me all you who are tired from carrying heavy burdens.)

◉ Mark 8:36–37 (Does a person gain anything by winning the whole world but losing sight of life?)

◉ Luke 6:24–26 (Those who are rich now will be poor later.)

◉ Luke 12:13–21 (A person's true life is made up of more than material possessions.)

NOTES

Use the space below to jot notes and reminders for the next time you use this strategy.

The Narrow Door

Jesus went through towns and villages on his way to Jerusalem, and this is what he told the people: "Do your best to go in through the narrow door." (Adapted from Luke 13:22–24)

The gate to life is narrow, and the way that leads up to it is hard." (Adapted from Matthew 7:13–14)

In your mind place yourself in the center of your bedroom. . . . Look around at all the familiar things—your furniture . . . your bed . . . pictures and books . . . stuff on the floor . . . your closet and its contents. . . . Open your closet. . . . Now open all the drawers in your room—one by one. . . . Take note of how much you have acquired in your short life. . . . Begin to collect all the things that you treasure, things that are meaningful and items that are necessary to you. . . . *[Pause for a few seconds.]*

Place these important things on your bed and look at the stuff of your life. . . . Have you included photographs? . . . music? . . . souvenirs? . . . books? . . . shoes and clothes? . . . jewelry? . . . a computer? . . . sports equipment? . . . a cassette or CD player? . . . Gather up the corners of the blanket on your bed and try to make a bundle that you can carry. Remove any objects that will not fit inside the blanket or cannot be carried. . . . *[Pause for a few seconds.]*

While holding your bundle, try to pass through your bedroom door. If the bundle is too large, too awkward, or too heavy, take a moment to lighten your load. . . . Now, with your bundle on your back, walk up or down stairs and through rooms and hallways until you reach the front door of your home. . . . If the bundle is still too large, stop and remove some more of its contents until you can pass through your front door and out to the street. . . . *[Pause for a few seconds.]*

You find a small car outside with its passenger door open. . . . Sit inside the car with your bundle on your lap. . . . If you cannot get your bundle into the car, open the blanket and remove more things until you can. . . . *[Pause for a few seconds.]*

The car takes you to your school. . . . Carry your bundle into your school building and through the halls until you reach your locker. . . . Open your locker and remove the things that are stored there. . . . Open your bundle and, one by one, place inside the locker the items you have been carrying . . . the things that are most important and necessary to you. . . . Close the locker door. . . . If everything does not fit inside the locker, decide what is most crucial or significant to you. . . . *[Pause for a few seconds.]*

And Jesus said to the people: "Do not store up riches for yourselves here on earth. . . . Instead store up riches for yourselves in heaven. . . . For your heart will always be where your riches are." (Verses 19–21)

"Be concerned above everything else with the Reign of God." (Adapted from Matthew 6:33)

Downside Up
and Upside Down:
Turning Around
to Beatitude Living

OVERVIEW
The aim of this hands-on exercise is to create a visible reminder that the Gospel message of God's justice is contrary to the order and priorities of contemporary society. By making a poster of the Beatitudes that forces readers to turn around physically, the young people create a symbol of the revolutionary message of the Gospel.

Suggested Time

About 20 minutes

Group Size

This activity is designed for at least two small groups of three to eight young people. If you have more than sixteen participants, create four or more small groups. You must have an even number of groups.

Materials Needed

- a Bible
- poster board
- markers
- scissors

☼ plain white paper
☼ cellophane tape or glue
☼ newsprint
☼ masking tape
☼ one or two mirrors

PROCEDURE

Preparation. Label the top of a sheet of newsprint, "Upside down." Label another sheet, "Downside up." On the first newsprint, list and number the nine opening clauses of the Beatitudes from Matt. 5:3–11—for example, write, "1. Blessed are the poor in spirit" (verse 3, NRSV). On the second sheet, list the corresponding nine conclusions to the Beatitudes—for example, write, "for theirs is the kingdom of heaven" verse 3, NRSV). Post the newsprint lists next to each other in the meeting room.

1. Recruit one or more volunteers to read the Sermon on the Mount from Matt. 5:1–12. Briefly discuss how this core teaching challenges us to organize our world differently and how Jesus calls us to experience God's justice by becoming like and being with beatitude people. Note that the Beatitudes turn our society and its priorities upside down and challenge us to turn around to God's way of seeing and being.

2. Divide the participants into an even number of small groups, with three to eight people in each group. Give each group one sheet of poster board, markers, scissors, plain white paper, and cellophane tape or glue.

Pair up the small groups. Assign one group in each pair to label its poster board, "Upside down," and work with the opening clauses to the Beatitudes. Assign the other group in each pair to label its poster board, "Downside up," and work with the Beatitude conclusions.

Point out the two newsprint lists that you created before the session, and announce that the groups will have 10 minutes in which to make a creative poster of the Beatitudes clauses that they have been assigned. Explain that their poster should force the reader to turn around or upside down in order to read the message. You might offer these examples of ways to do that:

Write words or phrases on plain white paper and tape or glue the paper to the poster upside down.

Write the letters in reverse order.

Use a mirror to help you write the clauses backward.

Write every other word upside down or backward.

Note that each poster should display a mind-boggling composition of the beginning or ending clauses from the Beatitudes. Make one or two mirrors available for groups that would like to use one.

3. When the groups have completed their work, post the creations of the paired groups together so that their message is complete. The end result for each pair of groups should be a series of nine Beatitudes written in a format that forces the reader to bend, stoop, and turn around in order to comprehend the message. Give the young teens a chance to look at the work of other groups.

4. Briefly discuss the young people's reactions to the exercise and ask why they think you had them create their posters this way. Comment that the actions of turning around and bending in order to read makes quite clear the Gospel message that Jesus preached a new and different way of living.

ALTERNATIVE APPROACHES

◎ The same exercise can be conducted using the sets of four blessings and four curses in the version of the Beatitudes in Luke's Gospel (6:20–26). The blessings and curses clearly show how Jesus' message turns the downside up (such as blessing the poor and persecuted) and the upside down (cursing the wealthy and comfortable).

◎ Begin step 2 by forming nine small groups, and give each group one of the Beatitudes and one strip of poster board. Tell the groups each to illustrate their line in the upside-down, turned-around fashion described in step 2. When everyone is finished, lay the strips in a broad circle or spiral on the floor so that people have to literally walk a circular path and turn around in order to read the complete message.

◎ Mount the posters on stakes and put them around the parish grounds or in the parking lot. In this way the young teens can share with the whole community the conversion message they have learned.

◎ Invite a young person to use a mirror to write the Beatitudes in reverse on a sheet of paper. Add legible instructions that direct the reader to stand before a mirror holding the paper, and add the title, "Do you see the world as God does?" Consider including the scriptural connections that follow, or creating a separate sheet with those passages. Photocopy the sheet or sheets, and give everyone a copy to take home.

SCRIPTURAL CONNECTIONS

◎ Hos. 12:6 (Hold fast to love and justice.)
◎ Joel 2:12–13 (Repent and return to me.)
◎ Zech. 1:3 (Return to me, and I will return to you.)
◎ Mark 1:15 (The Reign of God is near.)
◎ 1 Cor. 13:12 (What we see now is like a dim image in a mirror.)

NOTES

Use the space below to jot notes and reminders for the next time you use this strategy.

A Justice Rosary

OVERVIEW   Using the symbol of the rosary, this strategy makes a connection between prayer and global awareness. The young people create a rosary and learn about and pray for the needs of people in the five populated continental regions.

Suggested Time

15 to 30 minutes

Group Size

This strategy can be done with any size group.

Special Considerations

Because some young Catholics may be unfamiliar with the rosary as a traditional form of prayer, you may wish to begin with a brief presentation. If so, pass a rosary around the group and allow time for the young people to ask questions.

Materials Needed

☼ a large map of the world or a globe
☼ 18-inch pieces of leather or jute cord, one for each person
☼ beads in five different colors, one of each color for each person
☼ a candle and matches

PROCEDURE

1. Using a map or globe as an aid, invite the young people to share their knowledge and awareness of the different peoples in different parts of the world. Ask them to name and locate the following five populated continental regions of the earth: the Americas, Africa, Oceania (Australia, New Zealand, and the central and southern Pacific islands, including Indonesia), Asia, and Europe. If time permits invite the young people to share what they know about the lifestyles and needs of the peoples in each of those different regions.

2. Introduce the rosary as a traditional prayer form that allows Catholics to call to mind and pray for the needs of people across the world. Announce that each person will make her or his own rosary bracelet. Give each person a cord and five beads of different colors. Explain that each bead represents the peoples of one of the five continental regions. For example, you might use the following colors:

◎ *Purple.* the Americas

◎ *Green.* Africa

◎ *Yellow.* Oceania

◎ *Blue.* Asia

◎ *Orange.* Europe

Direct the young people to string their five beads in the center of their cord, tying a knot before the first bead and after each subsequent bead to ensure that the beads stay in place. When completed the bracelet may be worn on the wrist or simply tied to make a continuous loop and held in the hand.

3. Make the following comments in your own words:

The traditional rosary has five decades, that is, five sets of ten beads. Each bead represents one Hail Mary. The decades are separated by single beads that each represent one Lord's Prayer. The recitation of the rosary is accompanied by meditation on the traditional mysteries of Jesus' life, death, and Resurrection.

The justice rosary we have made is simpler, having just one bead for each decade and one knot for each Lord's Prayer. This rosary may be prayed in a variety of ways. For example, each bead could represent one Hail Mary, or it could represent ten prayers.

Instead of contemplating the traditional mysteries, those praying the justice rosary are invited to call to mind the sufferings, the needs, and the hopes of God's people in each of the five populated continental regions of our world. This is the most important element of the justice rosary.

4. Conclude the meeting by praying the justice rosary as a group. Light a candle and begin by saying the Lord's Prayer together. Invite one person to choose a colored bead. Ask the young teens to share what they know about the peoples of the continental region represented by that bead, such as the names of the region's various nations, their struggles or conflicts, and their wealth and gifts.

Invite the group to pray the Hail Mary for the peoples of the chosen region, inserting the name of the region in the second half of the prayer as follows:

"Holy Mary, Mother of God, pray for us sinners" . . . and for the peoples of [name of the continental region] . . . "now and at the hour of our death. Amen."

Repeat this prayer, then pray the Lord's Prayer again and move on to another bead. Continue in this manner until the group has prayed through all the knots and colored beads.

ALTERNATIVE APPROACHES

◎ Help the young people make many justice rosaries, distribute them in the school or parish, and sponsor a day of prayer for world peace. They could also create a small card describing the justice rosary and how it is used.

◎ Create five small groups and give each group the task of researching news or background information about the peoples of one of the five populated continental regions. The research may be done between meetings, or during a meeting if you make newspapers, news magazines, and other resources available.

◎ Use this project at the beginning of Lent, and instruct the young people to take their rosaries home. Encourage the young people's families to talk about the needs of various peoples and pray for one continental region each week during Lent.

SCRIPTURAL CONNECTIONS

◎ Ps. 34:15–18 (God listens to the righteous.)
◎ Jer. 29:11–14 (When you pray, I will answer you.)
◎ Matt. 7:7 (Ask and you will receive.)
◎ Luke 18:1–9 (God will judge in favor of those who pray.)

NOTES

Use the space below to jot notes and reminders for the next time you use this strategy.

Who's on Top?
A Look at the World
from the Other Side

OVERVIEW

This hands-on activity challenges the young teens to look at the world from a new perspective. In creating a map that is a reversal of the standard view, the participants examine common perceptions about the division of power, wealth, and respect among the nations of the world.

Suggested Time

20 to 30 minutes

Group Size

This strategy can be done with any size group.

Materials Needed

- a basketball
- a globe
- a Bible
- a large map of the world
- masking tape
- poster board
- markers

PROCEDURE

Preparation. Display a globe in an obvious place in the meeting room. Post a large map of the world where everyone can see it.

1. Gather the young people in a circle. Toss a basketball around the group and ask the following questions:

Where is the top of the ball, and where is the bottom?

When we look at the basketball, can we see which part of it should point up?

How could we know which part of the ball should point up?

Does it make a difference which way we look at or hold the basketball?

Can a ball have a top or a bottom?

2. Take the globe you have displayed in hand. Ask these questions to help focus the meeting:

Where is the top of the world, and where is the bottom?

When we look at our world, is there a part that should point up?

How do we know which is the part that should point up?

Does it make a difference which way we look at our world?

Can a world that is round have a top or bottom?

Why is the world always shown—in pictures, maps, and globes—with the Northern Hemisphere at the top and the Southern Hemisphere at the bottom?

Can you name and describe the countries of the Northern Hemisphere?

Who made the first maps and globes and pictures of our world? What part of the world were these people from?

Where do you think the influence and power is to be found in our world, on the top or on the bottom?

3. Comment briefly on the artificial divisions that separate the wealthy nations of the Northern Hemisphere from the economically deprived countries located mainly in the Southern Hemisphere.

Read Luke 14:7–14 and reflect on how Jesus reminds us that to be great in God's eyes, we must choose to be humble and serve. Invite the young people to discuss the following questions:

Which does God value more: wealth, power, and success, or service, love, and compassion?

What parts of the world does God value more? Why?

What part of the world would God put on top?

4. Divide the participants into small groups of no more than ten people. Explain that each group will create a symbol to help others see the world from a new perspective. Point out the traditional world map that you posted before the session, and tell the young teens that they will design a new world map.

Give each group a sheet of poster board and markers. Instruct the groups each to copy the continents onto their poster board, but to turn the map upside down so that the Southern Hemisphere is at the top and the Northern Hemisphere at the bottom. They should label the continents, oceans, and countries so that the words are right-side up.

Invite the participants to complete the picture by including a title for their poster, adding a scriptural quote, and incorporating some thought-provoking questions or comments such as these:

Who is on top in your world?

Who comes first in your world?

What is your worldview?

Take a look at the world from the other side.

Let God turn your world upside down.

Post the completed maps, and give the young people a chance to look over the work of their peers.

5. Conclude the experience by reminding the young people that the earth belongs to God and is a home to be shared equally by all. Therefore, no one is really on top of the world.

Ask the participants each to choose silently the name of one southern or Third World country. Lead the group in a prayer that recognizes the needs of the people in developing countries and celebrates the gifts that they offer to the world as human beings created in the image and likeness of God. Invite the young people to contribute by naming the country they have selected.

ALTERNATIVE APPROACHES

◎ Encourage the groups to enhance their maps by using pictures from magazines to illustrate the perceived contrast between the two halves of the world, as well as the theological and spiritual similarities. For instance, they might attach pictures of cities and cars and electronic devices in the Northern Hemisphere, versus pictures of remote villages and animals and hand tools in the Southern Hemisphere, and add pictures of people sharing and serving one another in both hemispheres.

◎ For another perspective ask one group to turn its map on its side before writing in the names of the continents, countries, and bodies of water.

◎ Instead of forming groups and directing each of them to make a map of the entire world, divide the class into five groups, and ask each group to draw a different one of the five inhabited continental regions (see the strategy "Justice Rosary" for a list of those regions) on poster board, turn it upside down to label the region and its countries, and cut it out. Then assemble the inverted regions into a world map on a wall in a public area such as a school assembly hall or church gathering space. Label the oceans and other major bodies of water. Attach a sheet with a brief explanation and invite the young people to add scriptural quotes, questions, and comments about the way we see and value peoples in the different parts of our world.

SCRIPTURAL CONNECTIONS

◎ Gen. 1:27–31 (God created human beings in the image and likeness of God.)
◎ Matt. 25:40 (Whenever you do good for others, you do it for God.)
◎ Luke 9:48 (The least among you is the greatest.)
◎ Gal. 3:28 (There is no difference between people because of nationality, status, or gender.)

NOTES

Use the space below to jot notes and reminders for the next time you use this strategy.

Break the Chains

OVERVIEW

This hands-on prayer experience helps the young people make the connection between the personal and social dimensions of injustice. Using the motif of chains, they create links that name a personal experience of injustice and a related social reality.

Suggested Time

About 20 minutes

Group Size

This activity works best with a group of ten or more.

Special Considerations

Be sure to conduct this activity in a space large enough so that the participants can form a complete circle.

Materials Needed

- ☼ 1-by-11-inch strips of colored construction paper, two for each person
- ☼ markers, one for each person
- ☼ a candle and matches
- ☼ one copy of resource 6, "Just One, Living in an Unjust World"
- ☼ tape or a stapler
- ☼ a Bible

PROCEDURE

Preparation. You may want to recruit three young people to read the three parts of resource 6. If you do, cut the parts from the resource and give one to each reader.

Consider recruiting people to help attach the participants' chains in step 3 of the procedure.

1. Direct the young people to sit in a circle. Distribute two strips of construction paper and a marker to each person. Light a candle and invite the group to be silent and listen.

Read part A of resource 6. Ask the participants to write on one of their colored strips one or two words that describe an injustice they have suffered, such as being excluded, laughed at, put down, cheated, discriminated against, or overlooked.

2. Read part B of resource 6. Direct the young people to write on their other strip a specific situation of injustice in our world that concerns them, such as racism, war, mass killing, homelessness, hunger, or debt. Tell them to try to connect the social situation with the personal injustice they named on the other strip. For example, being excluded can be connected with poverty, being cheated with international debt, being put down with discrimination or racism, and being bullied or beaten with the violence of war.

Note: Some young teens may find it difficult to recognize how personal experiences of injustice are connected with social realities like poverty, hunger, war, and racism. You may choose to explore these connections a little more deeply with younger adolescents.

3. Direct the participants to wrap one strip around their left wrist. With the help of other adults or older teens, or volunteers from the group itself, tape or staple each person's strip to form a bracelet. Then tell the young people to wrap the second strip around their right wrist. Again with the assistance of other leaders, thread the loose link of the bracelet on each person's right wrist through the bracelet on a neighbor's left wrist, and secure it with tape or a stapler. If your helpers are volunteers from the group itself, connect them to the circle as soon as everyone else is attached. The result should be a paper chain linking everyone, wrist to wrist, around the circle.

4. Invite the group to reflect on the symbolism of the chains that bind them together. Comment that the chains represent the effects of personal and global injustice, from which no one is spared. We have all been victims of injustice. We have also committed acts of injustice at some time in our life. The chains reveal the truth that when one person is oppressed, we are all oppressed.

5. Read part C of resource 6. Then ask two young people to read the following scriptural passages. Because their wrists are bound, they may need someone to help them hold the Bible.

◎ Luke 4:18–19
◎ John 20:22–23

Comment that Jesus gives us the power to break the chains of injustice by forgiving others and reaching out. Stand in the center of the circle. Call each young person in turn by name, and invite him or her to stand up and reach out with hands outstretched, palms facing up. The paper chains will break each time a participant stands, until eventually the whole group is free.

6. Conclude the ritual with the Lord's Prayer. At the end, repeat the line "and forgive us our trespasses, as we forgive those who trespass against us." Remind the young people that because they have been forgiven the injustices they have committed, they have received the spirit of forgiveness, which allows them to forgive those who have hurt them and to reach out to others who are hurting.

ALTERNATIVE APPROACHES

◎ Direct the young people to make another paper chain with links illustrating the same personal and social injustices that they wrote on their wristbands. Hang this chain around a crucifix or along the wall of the youth room, classroom, or church building.

◎ Instead of asking the young people to write social injustices on their second slip in step 2, provide used newspapers and news magazines. Instruct the participants to cut out headlines to illustrate unjust situations and glue or tape those headlines to their strip.

◎ Enact the same chain-link ritual using strips of white fabric in place of paper. Rather than inviting the young people simply to hold out their arms and tear the chains, call them to stand and each unbind their neighbor to the right. Give the fabric strips to the participants as a reminder of the power of forgiveness.

◎ Direct the young people to create break-the-chains prayer cards by stapling fragments of old jewelry chains to index cards, and adding scriptural quotations or a phrase that challenges people to break the chains of injustice. Help them distribute the cards at a parish or school reconciliation service.

SCRIPTURAL CONNECTIONS

- ◎ Isa. 61:1 (God has sent me to proclaim release to the captives.)
- ◎ Jer. 30:8 (I will break the yoke and remove the chains.)
- ◎ Mark 11:25 (Forgive, and you will be forgiven.)
- ◎ Eph. 4:32 (Forgive one another as God forgives you.)

NOTES

Use the space below to jot notes and reminders for the next time you use this strategy.

Just One,
Living in an Unjust World

Part A: Just One

I am just one among many in our world.

I have been hurt by words. I know what it is to be excluded.

I have suffered the violence of hatred. I know what it means to be beaten down or
beaten up.

I have been cheated. I know what it is to have dignity or possessions stolen.

I have been falsely accused. I know what it is to be punished unfairly.

I have seen others take more than they need. I know what it is to need and to go
without.

I have been ignored, invisible, I know what it is not to be heard or listened to.

Part B: Living in an Unjust World

And there are others, millions, who are caught in cycles of poverty and debt

who are homeless, hungry, and deprived of health care

who are persecuted because of race or religion

who are the victims of violence, personal and national

who are jobless and despairing

who suffer in the slums of cities, camps, townships, or prisons.

Part C: A Just One

There is so much injustice in our world.

I am part of it and it is a part of me.

I am just one person, and what can just one person do?

If we are all chained and paralyzed by injustice, who can set us free?

How can we break the chains?

How can I be a just one living in an unjust world?

Just Kids *A* to *Z*

This strategy invites the young people to create a poster with an alphabetical listing of attitudes for just living. It also affirms the role of young adolescents in making the world a more just place.

Suggested Time

About 45 minutes

Group Size

This strategy can be done with any size group.

Materials Needed

- ☼ markers
- ☼ a large sheet of poster board, at least 24-by-36 inches
- ☼ a scissors
- ☼ a Bible
- ☼ masking tape

PROCEDURE

Preparation. In the center of a large sheet of poster board, write in thick block letters the words, "Just Kids." Make each letter at least 12 inches high and 2 to 3 inches wide. Carefully cut out the letters, leaving the words as holes in the poster board. Write on the poster, above the cutout letters, the word, "Are," in bold print. Hang the poster in a visible location.

On a wall or table, display the cutout letters so that they form the words "Just Kids."

1. Ask the young people to stand up or raise a hand if they have experienced any of the following situations:

Someone tells you, "You're just a kid!"

A clerk in a department store shadows and scrutinizes you.

You hear adults talk in sarcastic or demeaning ways about young people.

People talk down to you, like they do not think you know very much.

Invite one or two people to share their experience of being considered "just a kid."

2. Make markers available, and direct the participants to sign their names boldly on the back of the cutout letters you have displayed in the meeting room, in recognition that they have each experienced being labeled by society as "just a kid."

3. Read 1 Tim. 4:12. Then make the following comments in your own words:

Society may view people your age as "just *kids.*" However, as young Christian disciples and with the right attitudes, you can become examples of just living—that is, you can become "*just* kids."

The Scriptures tell us that many of the heroes and prophets of our faith were called to leadership when they were just kids—such as David, Samuel, Mary, Jesus, John the Apostle, and Timothy. The same was true for Saint Brigit and Saint Patrick of Ireland, Saint Francis and Saint Clare of Assisi, Saint Joan of Arc, and many others.

4. Ask the group to describe some of the qualities of a just leader. You might want to start them off with an example or two like the ones that follow:

Just kids are aware—they think globally and act locally.

Just kids are connected—they work together.

After hearing some of their thoughts, introduce the idea of a poster with an alphabetical listing of just attitudes for just kids. Tell them that they will identify words or phrases that define a just attitude and write them on the poster. Each characteristic may be accompanied by a brief explanation.

Go through the alphabet with everyone together and solicit responses for each of the twenty-six letters, or divide the participants into small groups and distribute the letters among them. Write the words and phrases the young people come up with in alphabetical order on the poster titled "Just Kids." The end product should be a poster that is covered with an alphabetical array of adjectives and phrases that describe the qualities of just living.

5. Hang the poster in a parish or school gathering area with the cutout letters above it so that the title reads "Just Kids Are Just Kids."

ALTERNATIVE APPROACHES

◎ Create a card with all the alphabetical phrases suggested by the group. Make a copy of the card for everyone in the group, as a reminder never to be anything less than a just kid. You might also make copies for families in the parish to use with younger children, or to distribute at events like Confirmation or on World Youth Day.

◎ Have the alphabetical "just kids" list professionally printed on a poster or a T-shirt. Use the poster or shirt to generate awareness and support for youth outreach activities.

◎ Instead of doing the alphabetical "just kids" list all at once, start it with one or two letters at the first meeting of your group, and add to it at subsequent meetings until you have covered the entire alphabet.

SCRIPTURAL CONNECTIONS

◎ 1 Sam. 3:1–10 (The boy Samuel is called by God.)
◎ 1 Sam. 16:1–13 (David is anointed.)
◎ Matt. 11:25–27 (God has shown the unlearned what has been hidden from the wise.)

NOTES

Use the space below to jot notes and reminders for the next time you use this strategy.

Lenten Justice Crosses

OVERVIEW Through this hands-on project, the young people help spread the Lenten message of conversion to justice. They also become familiar with the message of the prophet Micah and the traditional spiritual disciplines of prayer, fasting, and almsgiving.

Suggested Time

30 to 40 minutes

Group Size

This strategy can be done with any size group.

Materials Needed

- ☼ newsprint and markers
- ☼ craft sticks, two for each person
- ☼ light-colored acrylic paints, and paintbrushes (optional)
- ☼ thin-line markers, one for each person
- ☼ wood glue or household white glue
- ☼ thin cord, string, or yarn
- ☼ scissors

PROCEDURE

Preparation. It may be helpful to make one cross, as described in steps 3 and 4, to show the participants.

1. Introduce the activity by reading the following scriptural quote:

"God has told us what is good, and what is required of us is this: to do what is just, to show constant love, and to live in humble fellowship with our God" (adapted from Mic. 6:8).

2. On newsprint write the three commands that you just read from the prophet Micah: "Act. Love. Walk justly." Invite the young people to reflect on the three attitudes that put us right with God. Note that during Lent we are called to act, love, and walk in ways that do justice to God.

On the same newsprint, write the following three commands: "Fast. Pray. Give away." Comment that especially during Lent, Christians are called to do justice to others through the traditional practices of fasting, praying, and almsgiving. Some of the young adolescents may be unfamiliar with the traditional disciplines of fasting and almsgiving. It may be helpful to describe those practices as spiritual exercises that we do for the soul, along with prayer. Add that those kinds of practices help us to become disciples.

Explain to the young people that they will be making simple crosses that communicate this Lenten message of justice. If you have prepared a sample cross, show it to the group.

3. Give each person two craft sticks, such as those that come in Popsicles. If you choose, direct the young people to paint their craft sticks. Allow the sticks to dry before proceeding with the project. Then make available thin-line markers; glue; thin cord, string, or yarn; and scissors. Lead the participants through the following process:

1. Carefully place one stick on top of the other to make a cross. Holding the cross in the center, mark where the sticks will later be overlapped and glued. Before you glue the sticks together, you will write some words on them. Be careful not to write any part of those words in the overlap area you have marked.
2. Write the word, "Act," on the left side of the horizontal crossbeam. Write the word, "Walk," on the right side.
3. On the top part of the vertical beam, write the word, "Love." On the bottom part, write the word, "justly."
4. Turn both sticks over.
5. On the left side of the horizontal beam, write the word, "Fast." Write the word, "Pray," on the right side.
6. On the top part of the vertical beam, write the word, "Give." On the bottom part, write the word, "away."

4. Direct the young people to glue their sticks together. When the sticks are dry, tell the participants to carefully wrap and tie a piece of thin cord, string, or yarn around the area of overlap. Then direct them to add a light coat of glue over the cord, string, or yarn.

5. Conclude the activity by inviting group members to choose one of the words on the cross and tell the group how they will make a commitment in that area to do justice to God and others during Lent.

ALTERNATIVE APPROACHES

- Provide adequate materials so that the young people can each create a number of the Lenten crosses, and then arrange for them to distribute the extra crosses at a parish or school liturgy on Ash Wednesday.
- The six commands of the justice cross can be used as themes for the six weeks of Lent. Create the cross throughout the Lenten season. Each week have the young teens add a different command to the cross and challenge them to find one way of doing justice in their world by living that command.
- Schedule this activity for the first week in Lent. Then hang the young people's crosses on a small tree or branch displayed in the meeting room. At each gathering during Lent, ask the participants to write on a strip of paper an example of how they have practiced one of the justice disciplines. Invite them to glue their strip on their cross next to the corresponding command.
- Help the young teens make one large justice cross and hang it in the parish gathering space. Provide blank strips of paper and tacks. Each week during Lent, invite the people in the parish to write on the paper strips ways they have lived out one of the commands and to attach the strips to the cross.
- Encourage the young people to take the message home by making a Lenten justice cross for each member of their family.

SCRIPTURAL CONNECTIONS

- Isa. 57:15 (God is a high and holy God who lives with people who are humble and repentant.)
- Matt. 6:5–7,16–18 (Jesus teaches about prayer and fasting.)
- Luke 9:23 (Take up your cross every day and follow Jesus.)
- 1 Cor. 13:3 (If you give away everything but have no love, it does you no good.)

NOTES

Use the space below to jot notes and reminders for the next time you use this strategy.

The Magnificent Seven: Seven Major Lessons of Catholic Social Teaching

This creative strategy challenges the young adolescents to illustrate seven radical social teachings of the Catholic church. By designing a series of posters, the young people create a colorful display that connects and contrasts the justice tradition of our faith with the realities of injustice in the world.

Suggested Time

About 60 minutes

Group Size

This strategy can be done with a group of seven or more young people.

Special Considerations

The lessons outlined in this strategy have been greatly summarized and represent only some of the key principles of Catholic social teaching. Because some young adolescents and even adults may be unaware of that teaching, you may choose to begin with a broader presentation on its principles. Background on that topic can be found in the *Catechism of the Catholic Church,* by the Libreria Editrice Vaticana, translated by the United States Catholic Conference (USCC) (Washington, DC: USCC, 1994), part 3, chapters 1 and 2, particularly numbers 1877 to 1948.

Materials Needed

- ☼ one copy of resource 7, "Seven Lessons for Our Time," cut apart as scored
- ☼ seven sheets of poster board
- ☼ markers
- ☼ a variety of used magazines
- ☼ glue or tape
- ☼ scissors
- ☼ two wooden dowels, each about 8 feet long
- ☼ tape, wood glue, or nails

PROCEDURE

Preparation. Using tape, wood glue, or nails, fasten two long dowels together to form a cross.

1. Divide the young people into seven task groups. When they are settled, read the following scriptural passage:

"I myself will teach your people and give them prosperity and peace. Justice and right will make you strong. You will be safe from oppression and terror" (adapted from Isa. 54:13–14).

Note that the Catholic church teaches principles for our time that are rooted in God's plan for peace and justice for all people. Emphasize that those principles directly challenge the realities of injustice in our world.

2. Announce that each group will be given one of seven justice principles of the Catholic church. The groups are to illustrate their assigned principle with words, pictures, and drawings and show how it contradicts unjust practices of our time. Emphasize that by creating this display, the young people will become teachers of justice.

3. Give each group one part of resource 7. Ask for a volunteer in each group to read from the group's lesson the church principle and the accompanying world practices. Briefly discuss how each lesson challenges the social realities of our time.

4. Give each group one sheet of poster board, markers, some used magazines, glue or tape, and scissors. Suggest that the group members take a few moments to discuss how they will illustrate their lesson on the poster. Tell them to begin by writing on the poster, in large bold letters, the words of the church principle. Challenge them to be creative in illustrating both what the church teaches and how the world contradicts that teaching. Allow 20 to 30 minutes for the groups to create their posters.

5. When the posters are finished, invite the groups to present and explain them. Afterward attach two posters on each arm of the cross that you made before the session, and the remaining three posters down the vertical rod.

6. Discuss with the young people which of the lessons they believe is most needed in our time. Close with a prayer, asking for God's help to spread that message of justice. Choose a public location in the school or parish to display the posters on the cross.

ALTERNATIVE APPROACHES

- Instead of making a large cross to display the seven posters, use string to bind the posters into an oversized book and cover the book with a title poster that reads, *The Social Gospel.*
- Invite the groups to make sandwich boards instead of posters. Direct them to illustrate their assigned justice principle on one side and the corresponding realities of injustice on the reverse side.
- Extend the themes of this exercise to cover seven sessions focusing on Catholic social teaching. Consider using some of the other strategies from this manual to expand the sessions. For example, the strategy "Who's on Top? A Look at the World from the Other Side" could be used with lesson 2 or 3.

SCRIPTURAL CONNECTIONS

- Gen. 1:31 (God looked at all of Creation and was pleased.)
- Isa. 61:8 (God loves justice and will make a covenant with those who are just.)
- Amos 5:24 (Let justice flow like a river.)
- Matt. 5:9 (Blessed are those who work for peace.)
- Luke 4:18–19 (Jesus was anointed by the Spirit to bring good news.)

NOTES

Use the space below to jot notes and reminders for the next time you use this strategy.

Seven Lessons for Our Time

Lesson 1

Catholic church principle. Life is sacred, and the dignity of the human person is to be respected.

World practices. capital punishment, legalized abortion, materialism, pornography, unrestrained commercialism and consumerism, drug trafficking and abuse

Lesson 2

Catholic church principle. All people are equal and have the right to participate fully in the life of their community.

World practices. individualism; class divisions and stereotyping; gender discrimination; ethnic, racial, and religious intolerance; neglect of immigrants and refugees

Lesson 3

Catholic church principle. All people are to be afforded human rights and challenged to live up to human responsibilities.

World practices. institutionalized racism, neglect of minority communities, ethnic genocide, imprisonment of political dissidents, abuse of prisoners, denial of political and social freedoms

Lesson 4

Catholic church principle. We are called to emulate God by showing a special preference for those who are poor and weak.

World practices. neglect of those who are poor, those who are older, women, and children; lack of affordable housing and medical care for those who are needy; a growing gap between impoverished and wealthy people and nations

----

Lesson 5

Catholic church principle. We work to continue God's plan for the earth. Work is dignified when workers' rights are protected and the economy serves the needs of all people.

World practices. displacement of people from their land, widespread unemployment and underemployment, unjust labor practices, low wages in impoverished countries, sweatshops, child labor, global systems of economic injustice

----

Lesson 6

Catholic church principle. We belong to a global family and are challenged to promote peace and solidarity.

World practices. nationalism and economic competition, ethnic division, persecution of minority populations, small- and large-scale conflicts, gang violence

----

Lesson 7

Catholic church principle. We share one planet; we are stewards of God's garden earth.

World practices. environmental destruction, loss of habitat for creatures and people, unsustainable consumption of global resources

----

(The seven Catholic principles summarized here are drawn from *Sharing Catholic Social Teaching: Challenges and Directions,* by the National Conference of Catholic Bishops [Washington, DC: United States Catholic Conference (USCC), 1998], pages 23–27. Copyright © 1998 by USCC, Washington, D.C.)

Doing Justice to Service: Transformative Outreach Activities

This strategy suggests a spiritual framework for service activities and some creative ways to engage the young people in outreach experiences that are transformative. Based on the understanding that we become seekers of justice through experiences of service, those ideas are aimed at connecting the young people, on a spiritual level, with those who are on the edges of their world, giving names and faces to realities of injustice and need.

Suggested Time

Outreach experiences can be tailored to a variety of time periods ranging from 2 hours to a week or more. It is difficult to develop effective and meaningful service experiences that require less than 1 to 2 hours.

Group Size

Outreach ministry with young adolescents takes place ideally in small groups of between five and ten young people under the guidance of one or two adults. Small groups increase the potential for the participants to make personal connections and may enhance the quality of the sharing after the event.

PROCEDURE

Choose a Focus

One helpful image for defining service is that of a pilgrimage, a quest to uncover the face of God or encounter Christ. This quest has two distinct movements: *out*reach (an outer journey to connect with a situation of need) and *in*reach (an inner journey of reflection and prayer that investigates the meaning and implications of the experience). Both movements require attention and preparation.

Outreach involves crossing personal and social boundaries. In every city and county, one can find borders of every kind to cross, including those that surround prisons, shelters, the homes of shut-ins, nursing homes, hospitals, and facilities for refugee and immigrant populations. Here are some questions you can ask yourself to help shape and discern a particular outreach activity:

- God, to whom should we go?
- Where are the boundaries that the young people need to cross?
- Where would Christ be found today?
- Where would Jesus take the young people today?
- Who would Jesus want them to know and be touched by?

Step into Service with Care

Once you discern the path the pilgrimage will take, it is necessary to plan the best possible use of the time available so that the experience will have the greatest possible effect on the young people. Following are ten guidelines for broadening and deepening an experience of outreach for young teens:

- *Plan it!* Match the gifts of the young people and the needs and opportunities for service available in your area.
- *Choose it!* Look for the margins, that is, opportunities for personal connection that will challenge, question, and clarify a young person's faith.
- *Prepare it!* Organize the logistics for the service component of the project, and also be sure to organize prayer, scriptural connections, music, a theme, symbols, reflections, and a rationale for the experience.
- *Make it connect!* Ensure that you and the young teens meet people in the service area, introduce yourselves and accept introductions, and politely ask questions.
- *Learn something!* Help the young people collect information about the life experiences, needs, and issues of the people being served.
- *Reflect on it!* Gather with the young people after the event, to share memories, impressions, prayer, and reflections on the experience and its implications.
- *Revisit it!* Frequently bring the experience to prayer or sharing at subsequent youth gatherings or liturgies. Encourage the young people to send thank-you cards and plan a return trip to deepen the relationship.

◎ *Value it!* Refer often to the issues that the young people encountered in their outreach project.

◎ *Vary it!* Ensure that the experience engages the whole person with activities for the hands, thoughtful discussion for the head, and prayer and faith sharing to touch the heart.

◎ *Spread it!* Invite the family and the parish to be transformed with you and the young people.

Deepen the Experience

Service becomes prophetic when it challenges the young people to readjust how they think and act and what they believe as Christians. The following questions may be valuable for concluding or deepening an outreach experience:

Why do you need to serve?

Why were you there, and who was with you?

What did you see and hear?

Who did you meet, and what did you feel like?

What happened to you as you served?

How were you served?

Whose company did you keep, and what did that person or persons teach you?

What connections did you make?

What difference did your serving make to you or others, and who will serve tomorrow?

Why are there suffering and needy people?

Where did you see the face of Christ?

What report will you take to God in prayer?

SUGGESTED STRATEGIES

Random-Acts-of-Kindness Cards

Group acts of kindness such as wiping windshields, cleaning alleys, mowing lawns, and sweeping sidewalks can be transformed by leaving reminders of the gift of service. Guide the young people in making cards that inform the recipients of the gift they have been given and invite them to pass on the act of kindness.

Light-the-World and Afterglow Rituals

Ritual and prayer provide a framework for outreach. Give small candles to each individual or service group, and focus on sharing light in a prayerful opening ritual and concluding reflection for the service activity.

Diaries of Young Prophets

Prayer and reflection are deepened when the young people are challenged to write their thoughts, memories, and prayers quietly in a journal. Distribute small blank notebooks and encourage the participants to use them as creative diaries that may later be shared with the parish or school.

Bridge Builders

Outreach provides excellent opportunities for the young people to span social, religious, and ethnic divides. Help your group connect with a church or youth group of a different denomination or with young people from different economic neighborhoods, in order to transform your outreach into justice building.

Prophetic Profiles

Service activities are transformed into experiences of justice when a relationship is formed. Suggest that young people who are active at social service agencies such as soup kitchens, shelters, and hospitals develop their relationships with staff and clients by interviewing them and sharing their stories in youth newsletters, bulletins, and Catholic papers.

Bread of Life

Sharing food is an important symbol for service and outreach. Rather than simply asking the young people to serve a meal at a community kitchen, deepen the experience by inviting them to share the meal. Also consider encouraging them to contribute to the meal by baking bread to share.

Prophetic Postcards

The young people can become prophets by inviting others to share in their outreach. Help them to create postcards from photographs of service activities, and to use the cards to invite other young people and adults to join them in serving others.

SCRIPTURAL CONNECTIONS

- Joel 2:28 (I will pour out my spirit on everyone so that they will proclaim my message.)
- Matt. 20:26–28 (If a person wants to be great, that person must be the servant of the rest.)
- John 12:26 (Whoever wants to serve me must follow me.)
- Gal. 5:13 (Serve one another in love.)

NOTES

Use the space below to jot notes and reminders for the next time you use this strategy.

Appendix 1
Connections to the Discovering Program by HELP Strategy

"Label Makers"

As presented, this strategy complements the following Discovering courses:
- *Becoming Friends*
- *Learning to Communicate*
- *Seeking Justice*

"The Peacemaker Award: In Recognition of Gospel Greatness"

This strategy may be used with any course in the Discovering Program, especially the following three:
- *Being Catholic*
- *Exploring the Story of Israel*
- *Seeking Justice*

"Youth Can"

This strategy may be used with any course in the Discovering Program, especially the following two:
- ◎ *Being Catholic*
- ◎ *Seeking Justice*

"A Place at Our Table"

As presented, this strategy complements the following Discovering course:
- ◎ *Seeking Justice*

"Peacebreak: A Calendar of Peace and Justice"

As presented, this strategy complements the following Discovering courses:
- ◎ *Being Catholic*
- ◎ *Seeking Justice*

"Christian Coupons"

As presented, this strategy complements the following Discovering courses:
- ◎ *Being Catholic*
- ◎ *Seeking Justice*

"Commercial Sing-Off"

As presented, this strategy complements the following Discovering course:
- ◎ *Seeking Justice*

"The Cost of Living"

As presented, this strategy complements the following Discovering course:
- ◎ *Seeking Justice*

"Good Sam Guide: A Hometown Survival Manual for Life in the Streets"

As presented, this strategy complements the following Discovering course:
- ◎ *Seeking Justice*

"Join the Dots"

As presented, this strategy complements the following Discovering courses:
- *Becoming Friends*
- *Meeting Jesus*
- *Seeking Justice*

"Mercy Works: The Hands-on Gospel"

As presented, this strategy complements the following Discovering courses:
- *Being Catholic*
- *Meeting Jesus*
- *Seeking Justice*

"The Eyes Have It"

As presented, this strategy complements the following Discovering courses:
- *Making Decisions*
- *Seeking Justice*
- *Understanding Myself*

"The Narrow Door: A Guided Meditation"

As presented, this strategy complements the following Discovering courses:
- *Meeting Jesus*
- *Praying*
- *Seeking Justice*

"Downside Up and Upside Down: Turning Around to Beatitude Living"

As presented, this strategy complements the following Discovering courses:
- *Exploring the Bible*
- *Seeking Justice*

"A Justice Rosary"

As presented, this strategy complements the following Discovering courses:
- *Being Catholic*
- *Praying*
- *Seeking Justice*

"Who's on Top?
A Look at the World from the Other Side"

As presented, this strategy complements the following Discovering course:
◎ *Seeking Justice*

"Break the Chains"

As presented, this strategy complements the following Discovering courses:
◎ *Dealing with Tough Times*
◎ *Praying*
◎ *Seeking Justice*

"Just Kids *A* to *Z*"

As presented, this strategy complements the following Discovering courses:
◎ *Being Catholic*
◎ *Seeking Justice*
◎ *Understanding Myself*

"Lenten Justice Crosses"

As presented, this strategy complements the following Discovering courses:
◎ *Being Catholic*
◎ *Seeking Justice*

"The Magnificent Seven:
Seven Major Lessons of Catholic Social Teaching"

As presented, this strategy complements the following Discovering courses:
◎ *Being Catholic*
◎ *Seeking Justice*

"Doing Justice to Service:
Transformative Outreach Activities"

As presented, this strategy complements the following Discovering courses:
◎ *Being Catholic*
◎ *Seeking Justice*

Appendix 2

Connections to the Discovering Program by Discovering Course

Becoming Friends

These HELP strategies complement this course as they are presented:
- "Label Makers"
- "The Peacemaker Award: In Recognition of Gospel Greatness"
- "Youth Can"
- "Join the Dots"

Being Catholic

The following HELP strategies are especially suited for use with this course:
- "The Peacemaker Award: In Recognition of Gospel Greatness"
- "Youth Can"

These HELP strategies also complement this course as they are presented:
- "Peacebreak: A Calendar of Peace and Justice"
- "Christian Coupons"
- "Mercy Works: The Hands-on Gospel"
- "A Justice Rosary"
- "Just Kids *A* to *Z*"

◎ "Lenten Justice Crosses"
◎ "The Magnificent Seven: Seven Major Lessons of Catholic Social Teaching"
◎ "Doing Justice to Service: Transformative Outreach Activities"

Celebrating the Eucharist

These HELP strategies complement this course as they are presented:
◎ "The Peacemaker Award: In Recognition of Gospel Greatness"
◎ "Youth Can"

Dealing with Tough Times

These HELP strategies complement this course as they are presented:
◎ "The Peacemaker Award: In Recognition of Gospel Greatness"
◎ "Youth Can"
◎ "Break the Chains"

Exploring the Bible

These HELP strategies complement this course as they are presented:
◎ "The Peacemaker Award: In Recognition of Gospel Greatness"
◎ "Youth Can"
◎ "Downside Up and Upside Down: Turning Around to Beatitude Living"

Exploring the Story of Israel

The following HELP strategy is especially suited for use with this course:
◎ "The Peacemaker Award: In Recognition of Gospel Greatness"

This HELP strategy also complements this course as it is presented:
◎ "Youth Can"

Gathering to Celebrate

These HELP strategies complement this course as they are presented:
◎ "The Peacemaker Award: In Recognition of Gospel Greatness"
◎ "Youth Can"

Growing Up Sexually

These HELP strategies complement this course as they are presented:
◎ "The Peacemaker Award: In Recognition of Gospel Greatness"
◎ "Youth Can"

Learning to Communicate

These HELP strategies complement this course as they are presented:
- "Label Makers"
- "The Peacemaker Award: In Recognition of Gospel Greatness"
- "Youth Can"

Making Decisions

These HELP strategies complement this course as they are presented:
- "The Peacemaker Award: In Recognition of Gospel Greatness"
- "Youth Can"
- "The Eyes Have It"

Meeting Jesus

These HELP strategies complement this course as they are presented:
- "The Peacemaker Award: In Recognition of Gospel Greatness"
- "Youth Can"
- "Join the Dots"
- "Mercy Works: The Hands-on Gospel"
- "The Narrow Door: A Guided Meditation"

Praying

These HELP strategies complement this course as they are presented:
- "The Peacemaker Award: In Recognition of Gospel Greatness"
- "Youth Can"
- "The Narrow Door: A Guided Meditation"
- "A Justice Rosary"
- "Break the Chains"

Seeking Justice

The following HELP strategies are especially suited for use with this course:
- "The Peacemaker Award: In Recognition of Gospel Greatness"
- "Youth Can"

  These HELP strategies also complement this course as they are presented:
- "Label Makers"
- "A Place at Our Table"
- "Peacebreak: A Calendar of Peace and Justice"
- "Christian Coupons"
- "Commercial Sing-Off"

- "The Cost of Living"
- "Good Sam Guide: A Hometown Survival Manual for Life in the Streets"
- "Join the Dots"
- "Mercy Works: The Hands-on Gospel"
- "The Eyes Have It"
- "The Narrow Door: A Guided Meditation"
- "Downside Up and Upside Down: Turning Around to Beatitude Living"
- "A Justice Rosary"
- "Who's on Top? A Look at the World from the Other Side"
- "Break the Chains"
- "Just Kids *A* to *Z*"
- "Lenten Justice Crosses"
- "The Magnificent Seven: Seven Major Lessons of Catholic Social Teaching"
- "Doing Justice to Service: Transformative Outreach Activities"

Understanding Myself

These HELP strategies complement this course as they are presented:

- "The Peacemaker Award: In Recognition of Gospel Greatness"
- "Youth Can"
- "The Eyes Have It"
- "Just Kids *A* to *Z*"

Acknowledgments *(continued)*

The scriptural quotations marked NJB are from the New Jerusalem Bible. Copyright © 1985 by Darton, Longman and Todd, London, and Doubleday, a division of Bantam Doubleday Dell Publishing Group, New York. All rights reserved.

The scriptural quotations marked NRSV are from the New Revised Standard Version of the Bible. Copyright © 1989 by the Division of Christian Education of the National Council of the Churches of Christ in the United States of America. All rights reserved.

The scriptural material described as adapted is freely paraphrased and is not to be used or understood as an official translation of the Bible.

The data in handout 1 and resource 1 comes in part from *Catholic Social Teaching and Human Rights: An Educational Packet,* by Jane Deren, Marissa Maurer, and Julie Vieira (Washington, DC: Center of Concern, 1998), pages C-6, F-3, and F-4. Copyright © 1998.

The data in handout 1 and resource 1 also comes in part from *Celebrate Jubilee and Justice!* by the Center of Concern (Washington, DC: Center of Concern, 1999), pages 10–11. Copyright © 1999.

And the data in handout 1 and resource 1 comes in part from *Operation Rice Bowl Lenten Program,* by Catholic Relief Services (Baltimore, MD: Catholic Relief Services, 1998), pages 21–22.

The strategy "Join the Dots" is adapted from "Coloured Dot Game," in *Racism,* number 14 of the Youth Topics series, by Christian Aid (London: Christian Aid, n.d.), page 2. Used by permission.

The words of Saint Basil the Great on page 66 are quoted from *Peacemaking: Day by Day,* vol. 1, by Pax Christi USA (Erie, PA: Pax Christi USA, 1985), page 9. Copyright © 1985 by Pax Christi USA.

The words of the Hail Mary on page 75 are quoted from *Our Sunday Visitor's Catholic Almanac,* by Our Sunday Visitor Publishing Division (Huntington, IN: Our Sunday Visitor Publishing Division, 1999), page 282. Copyright © 1998 by Our Sunday Visitor Publishing Division, Our Sunday Visitor, 200 Noll Plaza, Huntington, IN 46750.

The portion of the Lord's Prayer on page 82 is quoted from the *Catechism of the Catholic Church,* by the Libreria Editrice Vaticana, translated by the United States Catholic Conference (USCC) (Washington, DC: USCC, 1994), number 2759. English translation copyright © 1994 by the USCC—Libreria Editrice Vaticana.

The seven Catholic principles summarized on resource 7 are drawn from *Sharing Catholic Social Teaching: Challenges and Directions,* by the National Conference of Catholic Bishops (Washington, DC: United States Catholic Conference [USCC], 1998), pages 23–27. Copyright © 1998 by USCC, Washington, D.C.